Praise for *W*

This is a great book. I know Dawn. I know her journey. She lived it. She knows how to walk through it. It's so tempting to focus on the temporal when we're scared, uncertain, and depleted. Dawn shifts our focus to the ONE. Knowing the names of the ONE who can help us in those moments of doubt, fear, uncertainty, and anger can be our anchor in the storm. He is the only ONE who can help us make sense of our journey. Through this book, Dawn masterfully guides us to know Him better. He gives us peace in the storm, guidance through the wilderness, and wisdom for the moment.
—Leslie Vernick, Speaker, Relationship Coach, and Author of the best-selling books, *The Emotionally Destructive Marriage* and *The Emotionally Destructive Relationship*

To know the deep love of God is to know who He is. Dawn Stephenson, draws her reader into the depths of God's love by revealing the truth of who He truly is by who He calls Himself in His beautiful Word. Life-giving, healing, and transformative, *Who Do You Say I Am?*, allows the reader to open his or her heart to the touch of the Divine. One can almost picture Jesus, reaching His hand into our chests and taking our hearts into His very own hands. Cooperate. Let Him restore your heart, bring it back to life and into sync with His. He doesn't want you to ever skip another beat. Dawn proves this by beautifully connecting her readers to the reality of who He is so that you can know the reality of who you are – the beloved of God.
—Heidi Scanlon, National Community Church, Pastor of Prayer

Every seasoned warrior knows that our spiritual battles are not won in our own strength. *Who Do You Say I Am?* reminds us that our power rests in praying God's names, declaring our victories, and then sharing our testimonies. Dawn Stephenson uses her own life story to illustrate this path to triumph from trauma woven together with the power of God's Word.

—Barbara Hollace, Author, Editor, Speaker,
Hollace Writing Services, Hollace House Publishing

As you travel the pages of the book *Who Do You Say I Am? Triumph through Trauma Praying God's Names* by Dawn Stephenson, the revelation of the power and authority of His name is demonstrated by revelation and experience. A clear vision in everyday terms introduces the power found within His name and authority. A must-read book for the believer wanting to know his position in our world.

—Keitha Story-Stephenson PhD,
BlueSky Wellness Center, SkyBlue Family Ministries

I found Dawn's devotional about praying God's Names to be very uplifting. I have many books on the names of God. Dawn doesn't just tell you about the divine names, she invites you, via questions and prayer activations, to walk with God in the experience of each name. This is an excellent book for sharpening your prayer life.

—Louis McCall, Author of *According to Your Word Lord, I Pray*

As the balm of Gilead brought healing to the Israelites, so too the names of God have the power to heal our bodies and souls. Join author, Dawn Stephenson, as she leads readers on a journey to flourishing and wholeness in *Who Do You Say I Am? Triumph through Trauma Praying God's Names.* While reading, I personally experienced God in fresh new ways and was empowered to battle victoriously against the enemy of my soul. I highly recommend this book to anyone longing to overcome trauma. Through the power of praying God's names, I have encountered the Lord on a new level.

—Kathleen Hoffman, Stephen Ministry Leader,
Mt. Bethel Church, Mt. Bethel, PA

Dawn is truly an advocate for the evangelically oppressed. Her loving and caring coaching has made a tremendous impact on my life. *Who Do You Say I Am?* is written with great passion and zeal. She points the way to our ABBA Father God. Dawn's book is brimming over with encouragement and hope! A God who sees . . . hears . . . loves . . . and understands us!

—Lorrie Roe, Coaching Client

WHO DO YOU SAY I AM?

Also by Dawn E. Stephenson

Choosing Fierce: The Making of a Frontline Warrior (2018)
Dawn E. Stephenson

The Art of Brave Living (2016)
Diane Cunningham
(Dawn E. Stephenson, Contributing Author)

Available on Amazon

Who Do You Say I Am?
Triumph Through Trauma

Praying God's Names

Dawn E. Stephenson

Who Do You Say I Am? Triumph Through Trauma Praying God's Names
Copyright 2020 Dawn E. Stephenson

All rights reserved. No part of this publication may be reproduced, stored in a retrieval system, or transmitted in any form by any means, electronic, mechanical, photocopying, recording, or by any information retrieval or storage system without the express written permission of the author except in the case of excerpts used for critical review.

For more information or to contact the author by email: dawn@choosingfierce.com

Scripture quotations taken from the Amplified® Bible (AMP), Copyright © 2015 by The Lockman Foundation. Used by permission. www.lockman.org; Scripture quotations taken from the (NASB®) New American Standard Bible®, Copyright © 1960, 1971, 1977, 1995, 2020 by The Lockman Foundation. Used by permission. All rights reserved. www.lockman.org; THE HOLY BIBLE, NEW INTERNATIONAL VERSION®, NIV® Copyright © 1973, 1978, 1984, 2011 by Biblica, Inc.® Used by permission. All rights reserved worldwide; The Passion Translation®. Copyright © 2017 by Passion & Fire Ministries, Inc. Used by permission. All rights reserved. thePassionTranslation.com The Passion Translation® is a registered trademark of Passion & Fire Ministries, Inc.;Scripture quotations marked MSG are taken from *THE MESSAGE*, copyright © 1993, 2002, 2018 by Eugene H. Peterson. Used by permission of NavPress. All rights reserved. Represented by Tyndale House Publishers, Inc.; Scripture quotations marked NLT are taken from the *Holy Bible*, New Living Translation, copyright © 1996, 2004, 2015 by Tyndale House Foundation. Used by permission of Tyndale House Publishers, Inc., Carol Stream, Illinois 60188. All rights reserved

Book cover design: Christine Dupre
Book design: Russ Davis, GrayDog Press www.graydogpress.com
Book editing: Barbara Hollace, www.barbarahollace.com

ISBN: 978-1-7345159-2-3

Printed in the United States of America

Dedication

To each of us who has come from a background of crisis and trauma. Most oftentimes, if you look back far enough, you can find a broken little beloved child who was unseen, unknown, unheard, and unloved.

This book is dedicated to

Each of Our Own
"Broken, Little Beloveds"
Listen . . . He's calling your name.
He's redeemed you.
You're His.
You're loved.
You're safe . . . finally!
Welcome Home!
Isaiah 43:1

Introduction

It's great to have you here! Settle in and make yourself at home on these pages. That's how I've envisioned them being used. A comfy chair, a great smelling candle, a warm beverage in your favorite mug, and the sounds of sweet instrumental music playing quietly in the background. An atmosphere fit to entertain God Himself!

Here's the thing. This book wasn't meant to be read on the fly between innings of a game, or waiting in the carpool line. One of the things that God has shown me is He loves to give us His very best, and our heavenly Father loves our very best in return. It is like savoring a fine meal.

I have found that when I create space in my schedule to honor God, He delights in showing up. My heavenly Father can't wait to reveal more of Himself to me. So set the stage, block the calendar, and open your heart to receive all that God has to give you. I guarantee, it's the difference between fast food, drive-through dining and a three-star Michelin restaurant dining experience. You won't be disappointed. Most of all, you will be well fed!

This book was designed for both the individual reader, like yourself, and to be used in a small group setting. In its pages you will find 10 names (out of the over 950 names in Scripture) of God, with five devotionals under each name. This would lend itself to a semester of study over ten weeks.

Additionally, you will note that there are Come Up Higher Questions attached to each day. They were designed to bring you into the presence of God to commune and communicate with God Himself through the indwelling Holy Spirit in us. For some of us, this is a new experience. It's a lot like dating actually. It takes time to cultivate the nuances of God's voice as He directs and speaks to you. Similar to dating, the more time we spend with someone, the better we get to know them. This is no different.

Spending time with the questions daily, dialoguing with the Holy Spirit, digging into God's Word, will give you an opportunity to develop those skills. I encourage you to let your level of excitement match His as you set out to learn more of Him and the many ways that God is revealed in His names.

I like to think of each name as a facet in a gorgeous diamond. Every which way God moves, the "name facet" catches His light and shines radiantly around Himself. Glorious!

Additionally, I've included some journaling, doodling pages. I find these pages to be extremely important when I am in listening mode. I like to jot down what I am hearing, or doodle a vision God is giving me. Perhaps the Lord is speaking a verse of scripture that correlates with His name . . . put it there in either word or picture. Sometimes, it's a song that comes to mind. Take time to write out the lyrics. His ways of communicating are endless. I wanted to make it easy for you to have a place to capture His voice.

Lastly, enjoy your time in these pages. It is my prayer for each of you that you are able to see God revealed in each of these names. That the Lord meets you and makes these names personal to you. Mostly, that you fall in love with Him in new and deeper ways. Because, Beloved, it is in the sacred space of that deepening love . . . that's where the healing begins.

This is where we triumph over trauma.

So let the journey begin with a simple question, "Who are You, Lord?" Enjoy!

~Dawn

Contents

The Warrior Within..............................ix

1) ABBA ~ Daddy 1
Aramaic word for Father in regard to personal relationship

2) Adonai 33
Lord, Master, Ruler, Owner

3) El Elyon 65
The Most High God

4) El Roi..97
The God Who Sees

5) El Shaddai................................129
The Mighty, All-Sufficient One

6) Elohim......................................161
Supreme or Mighty God, Creator, Relational God

7) Immanuel.................................193
God With Us

8) Jehovah Jireh 225
The Lord Will Provide

9) Jehovah Shalom.......................257
The Lord Is Peace

10) Jehovah Shammah........................289
The Lord Is There

Triumph Through Trauma.................321

Acknowledgments.............................331
About the Author..............................333
Author's Note....................................335

The Warrior Within

Humbly I Bow, Victoriously I Arise
A Declaration of My Identity In Christ

Humbly I kneel to surrender the wounds of my broken story
The tale of the wounded wounding
Today I return to the place my story began
ABBA, Who do You say I am?

Humbly I kneel to make You King
Today, Adonai, Mighty Master,
Today I receive the warrior's weapon of forgiveness
Today I extend that forgiveness to the ones who have wounded
Hate is simply too big a burden to carry
I honor the Imago Dei placed in me by You

Humbly I kneel to hand You my shame
El Elyon, God Most High,
In one glorious unbecoming
I receive my identity as Your own
The one who breaks through darkness
Has been consecrated to be victorious
Through You, I carry the victory of every battle
This is who You say I am
Today, I believe

Humbly I kneel to receive from You
El Roi, the belief that I am seen
I am acknowledged
I am welcomed at Your table
I am honored
I have a voice that is valued
I am heard
I am loved by The God Who Sees

Humbly I kneel in the presence of El Shaddai
Mighty and All Sufficient
To receive my belovedness
From the One who anoints me with His lavish grace

Victoriously I arise, a Valiant Warrior,
O Elohim, Scripter of my story,
To walk in the anointing of words
spoken over me in eternity past

Victoriously I arise,
God with me, in me, for me,
Immanuel
To carry the touch of the Divine

Victoriously I arise
Splendidly arrayed for battle
In the most magnificent spiritual armor
Straight from the hand of the God who provides
Jehovah Jireh

Victoriously I arise
To enter the sacred space of His peace
A mighty fortress
The place where all is whole, complete,
Nothing missing, nothing broken
The presence of Jehovah Shalom

Victoriously I arise
To take Your hand,
To wield the weaponry of Your presence
in every battle for my wholeness
O Jehovah Shammah
You are here
I am who You say I am
Today I believe
I am whole

Amen

ABBA
Daddy

Aramaic word for Father
in regard to personal relationship

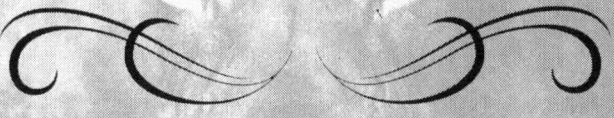

Humbly I kneel to surrender the wounds
of my broken story
The tale of the wounded wounding
Today I return to the place my story began
ABBA, who do You say I am?

Day One

Heaven: The Eternal Father's Day

FATHER'S DAY – FOR SOME, it is the elephant in the room. Take this day back if it has you tangled.

"How can I possibly do that?"

No matter what our triggers, issues, or memories are about this day, we can always give honor to our heavenly Father, ABBA, for all the richness and goodness He lavishes on us.

Honor is a word not often seen in today's culture, yet sorely missing as evidenced by the lack of it among cultures, races, and even political parties, but so often primarily amongst ourselves. All the way back to that small broken child who may have been critically dishonored, not treated with integrity. Let your heavenly Father restore honor to the little you. Let ABBA transfer that same honor to you in your present-day self. This is reverse engineering.

I pray that you go back and grab that sweet child, the broken, wounded, younger you and deliver that child directly into the healing arms of ABBA Father's perfect love. That today, perhaps for the first time, you would snuggle up on His lap and let Him lavish both the adult and child version of you with the same love that has been there since eternity past. Let it heal the insides of you as ABBA reminds you that He has never lost sight of you.

Then together with Him, may we lock arms and be "repairers of the breach" today, Beloved.

I am praying that on that day, and every day, you start by getting busy creating cultures of honor and integrity in both yourself and in your relationships with God and others.

I pray you spend some time in ABBA's lap today letting Him love on both the adult you and that sweet child version. Spend some time asking Him what needs to change in your life regarding honor and integrity, especially toward yourself. Ask Him to show you how to walk in your belovedness.

Then together with Him, may we lock arms and be "repairers of the breach." We can do that by creating cultures of honor and integrity in both ourselves and in our relationships with God and others. Can you do that? If not, speak these prayers over yourself until you can.

Prayers of Affirmation

ABBA, Today I crave the blessing and honor that walking with You brings to my life. As I walk alongside You with integrity of heart and uprightness, You bless that sacred space of unity with Yourself. Our unity commands a blessing. Thank you, ABBA, for desiring me so much that You made a way for me to have eternal access to You.
    Scripture Reference: I Kings 9:4-5, Psalm 133:3, John 3:16

ABBA, Today I receive the favor and honor that You have bestowed on me. As Your child, I receive the blessing, and every good thing that comes from my righteous walk with You. Thank you that Christ's work on the cross ensures that I am always able to walk in righteousness before You.
    Scripture Reference: Psalm 84:11, I Corinthians 1:30

ABBA, Help me to understand that Your love for me knows no limits, it is unconditional. When I have lost my way, You quickly drop everything to come and find me. Thank you, ABBA, for that kind of love. You are My Shield and My Defender.
    Scripture Reference: I Corinthians 13:7, Matthew 18:12, Psalm 18:2

Come Up Higher Questions

1) Based on Hebrews 10:35–39, Where have I cast away my confidence in Your name here, Lord?

2) Where am I specifically drawing back in my knowledge of this name, Lord, purposefully not looking at things I need to see? Open my eyes to any blind spots I have to You regarding this name. Confess what He shows you.

3) Where specifically am I in need of endurance regarding this name, Lord?

4) What lies have I been believing about You pertaining to this name, Lord?
   What lies have I been believing about myself pertaining to this name, Lord?
   Confess those lies by writing them down in the journal pages and offer them back to Him.

5) Ask Him what truths He would like to replace those lies with regarding this name. Write those down in the journal pages that follow.

Today's Scripture Reference

"Therefore, do not throw away Your confidence, which has a great reward. For you have need of endurance, so that when you have done the will of God, you may receive what was promised. For yet in a very little while, He who is coming will come, and will not delay. But my righteous one shall live by faith; and if he shrinks back, my soul has no pleasure in him. But we are not of those who shrink back to destruction, but of those who have faith to the preserving of the soul." —Hebrews 10:35–39 NASB

ABBA ~ Daddy

HEAVEN: THE ETERNAL FATHER'S DAY

Draw What's on Your Heart

Day Two

Arise – Walk Out the Fullness of Your Calling

SO HERE'S THE THING . . . God designed Himself to be known by you.

In the VERY beginning, we don't have to travel but to the third chapter of Genesis in verse 8 to see that every evening God came to walk daily with Adam and Eve in the cool of the day. Because He desired their company . . . because their heavenly Father loved them, just as much as He loves us.

Later in scripture, Paul also got to walk a short road piece with God. When ABBA decided it was time to turn a man's life around. Because, again, his heavenly Father loved Paul and desired his company.

So like each one of these scriptural giants, we are created and sought out by ABBA Father to keep company with Him. We are designed to walk with God while fulfilling our purpose and calling, which have also been lovingly designed by Him and tucked safely within each one of us.

Paul says it this way in Philippians 3:10 Amplified Bible Classic Edition: "[For my determined purpose is] that I may know Him [that I may progressively become more deeply and intimately acquainted with Him, perceiving and recognizing and understanding the wonders of His Person more strongly and more clearly], and that I may in that same way come to know the power outflowing from His resurrection [which it exerts over believers], and that I may so share His sufferings as to be continually transformed [in spirit into His likeness even] to His death, [in the hope]."

See the beauty of rising up, Beloved, is that you arise to the fullness of your calling in Him, that you would know Him intimately as you walk with ABBA Father. That you would perceive, recognize, and understand the wonders of the person of Christ, and that you would walk out your calling like Paul – finishing strong in the full operation of Jesus' resurrection power.

Can you receive that love for yourself today? If not, please repeat the following prayers over yourself until you can.

Prayers of Affirmation

ABBA, It is at Your name every knee bows. It is hard to comprehend that You are both infinite and intimate at the same time. I know that I am loved by You with an everlasting love. Today, despite my lack of understanding, and perhaps my unbelief, ABBA, I am choosing to receive Your love.
Scripture Reference: Philippians 2:10, Jeremiah 31:3, Job 36:26

ABBA, I desire to make room in my heart so You can come walk daily with me. Your plans for me are good, I receive them.
Scripture Reference: Genesis 3:8, Jeremiah 29:11

ABBA, You desire my companionship so much You gave Your only Son to ensure that I could enter into Your presence. Your desire for me is to come away with You and rest for a while. Just to keep me company – to heal me, to draw me to Yourself. Today, ABBA, I receive the blessing of Your presence, the pleasure of Your company, Your healing, and Your companionship.
Scripture Reference: John 3:16, Mark 6:31

Come Up Higher Questions

1) Lord, would You give me an opportunity to apply the knowledge of this name in my life today?

2) Lord, can You show me what You see in my applying this name today?

3) Lord, can You show me the treasure that You have placed in this person / situation in which I will be applying this name today?

4) What lies have I believed here that I need to break agreement with today in regard to this name / person / situation?

5) What truths do I need to replace those lies with?

Today's Scripture Reference

"But prove yourselves doers of the word, and not merely hearers who delude themselves. For if anyone is a hearer of the word and not a doer, he is like a man who looks at his natural face in a mirror; for once he has looked at himself and gone away, he has immediately forgotten what kind of person he was. But one who looks intently at the perfect law, and law of liberty, and abides by it, not having become a forgetful hearer but an effectual doer, this man will be blessed in what he does."

—James 1:22–25 NASB

ABBA ~ Daddy

Draw What's on Your Heart

Day Three

A Father's Love

It is the most precious thing to me to watch my three-year-old grandson work hard to emulate all things "Daddy." He eats, breathes, and studies his dad.

Watches how he eats, lives to play basketball and golf (just like Daddy), can't get enough of all the good food, and waits, peeking out the door for the sound of his daddy to open it. All so he can run and wrap himself around his legs.

As if by design . . . because it was.

Hardwired by our own heavenly ABBA Father, deep down in our very fibers, to be made, known, and loved by the two people who created us. It is such an integral part of our development.

When it goes wrong, and that story and design are disrupted, it goes really wrong! There are consequences of brokenness in that little person to be paid that can last a lifetime.

Enter ABBA Father. It's important He enters here. Because only the one who wrote the original script can come in and redeem it.

How wonderful to know that all the wounds handed to us when the model went sideways can be set straight and redeemed by ABBA Himself. He has the capacity, love, and ability to right all the wrongs . . . ABBA. Our heavenly Father gave His own son for the privilege to do so.

Beloved, it is my prayer that you KNOW and BELIEVE that your ABBA Father is who He says He is . . . the One who came to save that which was lost. To redeem our broken stories.

Can you trust Him to rewrite your story of brokenness that was handed to you by another? I pray you can. If not, repeat the prayers below until you can.

Prayers of Affirmation

ABBA, You love us with an everlasting love. You draw us to Yourself to redeem us with lovingkindness. Thank you for rewriting my story.
   Scripture Reference: Jeremiah 31:3

ABBA, Whom have I in heaven but You, Lord! I can't desire anyone more than You! You are the strength of my heart and my portion forever.
   Scripture Reference: Psalm 73:25

ABBA, You loved us enough to send Your only Son to die for us. Because we believe that, You have promised us eternal life with You and abundant life here.
   Scripture Reference: John 3:16, John 10:10

Come Up Higher Questions

1) How do I love You in truth today, Lord, in regard to this name?

2) Ask God if He can show you how to love yourself the way He loves you specifically in regard to this name.

3) In what tangible ways can I partner with this name of God to manifest Your presence more clearly in my daily life today, Lord?

4) What gift or talent (equipment or fruit of the Spirit) do I need to manifest this name of Yours on earth today, Lord?

5) Lord, is there anything more You would like to reveal to me about this name?

Today's Scripture Reference

"For the testimony of Jesus is the spirit of prophecy."
—Revelation 19:10b NASB

"But the fruit of the Spirit is love, joy, peace, patience, kindness, goodness, faithfulness, gentleness, self-control; against such things there is no law."
—Galatians 5:22-23 NASB

> "The most important thing a father can do for his children is to love their mother." —Theodore Hesburgh

ABBA ~ Daddy

A Father's Love

Draw What's on Your Heart

Day Four

A Sacred Trust

Like the first syllables rolling out of a baby's mouth, "Dada." The name Jesus calls His own Father (see Mark 14:36, Romans 8:15, Galatians 4:6). Jesus, the One who was making the way possible for us to know God the Father the same way Jesus knew God the Father, His own ABBA.

ABBA designed us to not only say His name first, but to be known by us first in the "type" of our earthly fathers . . . who were created to ultimately point us to our heavenly Father. Through our earthly father's tender loving care, discipleship, nurturing, protective guardianship of us that is how we learn ABBA – we have been placed in our earthly father's trust. It is truly a sacred stewardship in which ABBA places us, His Beloveds.

In other words, we learn ABBA (our heavenly Father) through our earthly parents (yes, we include mothers, as God embodies the fullness of both the male and female that He created. Most often, God is referred to in the male format).

We come hardwired by ABBA that way – to be nurtured, loved, and cared for by the two people who made us. Sometimes that works out and sometimes it doesn't. However, it doesn't eradicate the need, nor does it change who ABBA is . . . He remains the same.

Regardless of the way you "learned" ABBA on the earthly level from those entrusted with your care, He desires to be known to you as He actually is . . . right now.

To erase all the wounds of the "others." To show you tender loving care, discipleship, nurturing, protective guardianship to that which has been sacredly placed by you in His care . . . ABBA. Once He gets you to safety, He can get you to healing.

My prayer for you, Beloved, is that you call on ABBA and ask Him to reveal Himself to you in this very precious, very intimate way . . . a "Daddy" to that longing little child inside each of us.

Let ABBA bring you to safety . . . Let ABBA heal the wounds. ABBA sacrificed His only Son for the privilege to do so . . . Are you ready? Speak these prayers over yourself as you decide.

Prayers of Affirmation

For ABBA so loved me that He was willing to sacrifice His Only Son, Jesus, for me to have an eternal relationship with Him – to heal me in the now . . . to right all the wrongs. For Him to show me the perfect love of ABBA Father.
Scripture Reference: John 3:16

ABBA, I am loved with an everlasting, perfect love. You have drawn me to Yourself with that same unfailing love.
Scripture Reference: Jeremiah 31:3

ABBA, because I am Yours I am led in pathways of life, right into Your presence where there is fullness of joy and treasures at Your right hand. When I look to You, You make me radiant and unashamed.
Scripture Reference: Psalm 16:11, Psalm 34:5

Come Up Higher Questions

1) How can I use this name of God to bring the kingdom of heaven to earth today, Lord?

2) How does this name of God contribute to the flourishing of my neighbors and city, Lord?

3) Lord, can You give me an encouraging word for another regarding this particular name through picture, scripture, song, or word?

4) Ask Him for any further clarification on the above word that He would like to share with you. Write it down. Share these words with that person.

5) Lord, what would You like to say to me today regarding this name that might encourage my own heart? Write it down.

Today's Scripture Reference

"Your kingdom come, Your will be done on earth as it is in heaven."
—Matthew 6:10 NASB

"Behold, I will do something new, now it will spring forth; will you not be aware of it? I will even make a roadway in the wilderness, rivers in the desert."
—Isaiah 43:19 NASB

"ABBA. Once He gets you to safety, He can get you to healing."
—Dawn E. Stephenson, *Who Do You Say I Am?*

ABBA ~ Daddy

A Sacred Trust

Draw What's on Your Heart

Day Five

Too Loud!

I FELT THE FULL-FORCE body slam and tackle effect instantly – not much ensuing damage from a three-year-old. It was quickly followed by hands over his ears, a wild "no"–shaking head gesture, and wailing, "TOO LOUD, MOM . . . TOO LOUD!"

Who would have ever thought a fun-filled day at the county fair amidst the rides and food trucks could evoke such a dramatic response?

Seems my son's quieter world had been replaced by the "noise" of real life, courtesy of his recent ENT surgery. My son was now privy to new levels of peace-disrupting noise – shaking his previously silent surroundings. Sound familiar?

I'd say in the past few months we have all been privy to new levels of peace-disrupting noise . . . bombarding us from all sides, not to mention many fronts. The question becomes, how do we hold our precious peace in the midst of it all? Where do we run?

Enter ABBA! The endearing ancient Hebrew word for "Daddy." Not "Father", that would be too formal, austere. In moments like these, when the noise of life is closing in, we need "Daddy."

Let's take a read from the playbook of Jesus in Matthew 5, better known as The Sermon on the Mount. An interesting thing jumped right out at me in verse one, "When Jesus saw His ministry drawing huge crowds, He climbed a hillside."

Interesting response to a crowd that has come to see you . . . you leave!

But Jesus knew a thing or two, because He'd seen a thing or two. What He so often did in these circumstances, when life went into a "TOO LOUD, ABBA, TOO LOUD!" moment . . . Jesus ran to tackle His Father's legs. To sit quietly with His ABBA and allow Himself to be consoled and to recalibrate . . . for as long as it took to stabilize . . . to make sure that His prized inner-peace was protected. Sounds like the best plan of all. Even, or should I say, ESPECIALLY, when the crowds and pressures of life are pressing in.

That day at the fair it was a quick grab and a long hug and hold to assure my little guy that he was in a "new world" . . . one that was going to be a lot louder. But I was there. A set of ear plugs later, and we learned that the right tools in the right moment make the difference between winning and losing the thing.

Beloved, my prayer for you today is that you know enough to run to ABBA in this new, loud, and sometimes chaotic world in which we find ourselves. That you recalibrate at the feet of ABBA Himself until the Prince of Peace has returned to residency in your heart. Sound like a plan? If not, repeat these prayers over yourself until it does.

Prayers of Affirmation

ABBA, You sent Your only Son, the Prince of Peace, so that we might live in Your peace continually. I break partnership with anything that comes against that peace.
Scripture Reference: Isaiah 9:6

ABBA, You have promised to leave us Your peace through Jesus. This is Your not-of-this-world peace, but it is ours through Your Son. Lord, I receive that peace today.
Scripture Reference: John 14:27

ABBA, Today I choose to sit at Your feet in the secret place where I can adore You and worship You. Better is one day in Your courts than thousands elsewhere.
Scripture Reference: Psalm 84:10

Come Up Higher Questions

1) Lord, what is the heart of this name of God towards me today?

2) Lord, is there anything else about the heart of this name of God towards me that I need to know or do today?

3) Lord, is there any area in my life in regard to this name in which I am out of obedience or susceptible to sin? Confess that area in the journal space provided.

4) Lord, what is the gift that You desire to give me in place of that area of weakness or disobedience that I can use to build Your kingdom?

5) Lord, what aspect of Your character or nature would You like to show me, in regard to this name, that I have not seen before?

Today's Scripture Reference

"Therefore there is now no condemnation for those who are in Christ Jesus."
—Romans 8:1 NIV

"What then shall we say to these things? If God is for us, who is against us? He who did not spare His own Son, but delivered Him over for us all, how will He not also with Him freely give us all things?"
—Romans 8:31-32 NASB

"If we confess our sins, He is faithful and righteous to forgive us our sins and to cleanse us from all unrighteousness."
—I John 1:9 NASB

ABBA ~ Daddy

Too Loud!

Draw What's on Your Heart

Adonai
Lord, Master, Ruler, Owner

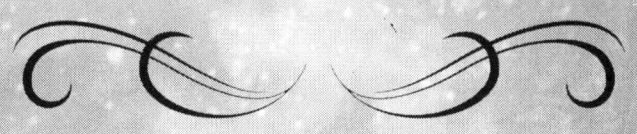

Humbly I kneel to make You King
Today, Adonai, Mighty Master,
Today I receive the warrior's weapon of forgiveness
Today I extend that forgiveness to the
ones who have wounded
Hate is simply too big a burden to carry
I honor the Imago Dei placed in me by You

Day One

Unshaken

DID YOU EVER WONDER how the battle is won? This . . . is how we win the thing – we remain UNSHAKEN.

"How is that even possible?" you may ask.

Enter Adonai – Lord, Master, Ruler, Owner.

Straight outta scripture. Watch how it works here.

Daniel 1:8 it's how we win the thing. "Daniel was resolved in his heart" or in my version, "Daniel MADE UP HIS MIND that he would not defile himself."

Then Daniel 1:9, "God granted Daniel favor and compassion."

See Daniel's reward? God's favor and compassion.

How does one remain UNSHAKEN!? You start by laying the firmest of foundations . . . "You resolve in your heart" that no one gets your full attention or affection except Adonai.

It's Daniel 1:8! It's as simple as making up your mind that this is what you are going to be doing, because that's how devoted Adonai is to you. We are locking eyes with Adonai and running fast towards Him as His heart melts at that dedication. Everything else can either bow down or get out of the way. All the way into the Lion's Den. That's a firm resolve.

Not easy to do in Daniel's surroundings. He was a Prisoner of War in a foreign land, 900 miles from home . . . as a young teenager. Yet his devotion to Adonai was non-negotiable. Even when the law said that to bow to anything except the King of Babylon was a death sentence. Daniel's response? He continued to go upstairs, open his window, and pray to Adonai. He did this not once, not twice, but three times a day. That's devotion.

Beloved, my prayer for you is that you remain UNSHAKEN! Even in the most unsettling surroundings. That's how we win the thing!

Are you ready? If not, repeat the following prayers over yourself until you are.

Prayers of Affirmation

Adonai, Today I will overcome by the blood of the Lamb, and the word of my testimony. Like Daniel, I will not shrink back even to the point of death.
Scripture Reference: Revelation 12:11

Adonai, I am trusting You, who loves me with Your life, to give me the strength I need to do all things that You have entrusted me to do today to accomplish Your will for my life.
Scripture Reference: Philippians 4:13

Adonai, I am safe within the walls of Your will for me. You hold me there and protect me. In You, I take refuge. Apart from You, I have no good thing.
Scripture Reference: Psalm 16:1-2

Come Up Higher Questions

1) Based on Hebrews 10:35–39, Where have I cast away my confidence in Your name here, Lord?

2) Where am I specifically drawing back in my knowledge of this name, Lord, purposefully not looking at things I need to see? Open my eyes to any blind spots I have to You regarding this name. Confess what He shows you.

3) Where specifically am I in need of endurance regarding this name, Lord?

4) What lies have I been believing about You pertaining to this name, Lord?
    What lies have I been believing about myself pertaining to this name, Lord?
    Confess those lies by writing them down in the journal pages and offer them back to Him.

5) Ask Him what truths He would like to replace those lies with regarding this name. Write those down in the journal pages that follow.

Today's Scripture Reference

"Therefore, do not throw away Your confidence, which has a great reward. For you have need of endurance, so that when you have done the will of God, you may receive what was promised. For yet in a very little while, He who is coming will come, and will not delay. But my righteous one shall live by faith; and if he shrinks back, my soul has no pleasure in him. But we are not of those who shrink back to destruction, but of those who have faith to the preserving of the soul."
—Hebrews 10:35–39 NASB

Adonai

Draw What's on Your Heart

Day Two

Stoke the Furnace

THINGS THAT COME from your children, especially regarding all things Jesus, hold a special place in a Momma's heart. This is one of them that was shared with me this week. So appropriate, so divine.

I have been camped in Daniel 3, where the furnace is burning several times hotter than normal . . . but not for the purpose of the little "k" king who built it.

See, here's the thing . . . while the little "k" king is dancing around in his pride and arrogance, making people bow and scrape at his name, Adonai sits in heaven watching. Having been the one to assign little "k" his part in the story from eternity past . . . because Adonai needed a hot fire.

"Step up to the plate, little "k", stoke the furnace for Me. I'm just getting started here."

Adonai's voice turns in little "k's" head, "If you would be so kind as to put the "Three Boys" in that fire, that would be great."

Here's the thing about Adonai . . . He made Himself at home in the hearts of "Three Boys" who knew Adonai as Lord, Master . . . not so much little "k". See it wasn't that Adonai didn't try, it's just that silly little "k" was busy, building statues of pride and arrogance to himself. No room for Adonai. Proverbs calls that "exalting yourself."

So stoke the fire, little "k". Usher "The Boys" on in. Close the doors and watch. You are about to become a player in the script of Adonai. Because Proverbs also tells us, God moves the hearts of kings and bends them to do what He wants.

Make no mistake today, Beloved, about your fire. No matter who lit the fire, stoked it hotter than hell itself, and proceeded to shove you in it and slammed the door, Adonai is the One who will meet you in those flames. He will walk with you there, Adonai will refine you like gold. That fire is His tool. Stay in it and don't rush out.

Because that fire, meant to bring you to your knees . . . has been hijacked by Adonai for His purpose in your life. Because you bent your knee to Adonai, that fire will purify you, it will strengthen you, it will make you reflect the image of the One who made you.

When you walk out of that fire, you will bear telltale markings that you have held court with Adonai amidst the flames. Your clothes will not be singed, you will not be burned, you won't have a trace of smoke smell around you. No trace of the flames . . . only Adonai with you, and in you, remains.

And here's the best part . . . that very fire, meant to bring you to your knees . . . brought the little "k" to his knees . . . in repentance.

Walk in the fire today, Beloved, with Adonai. Let the fire do its work.

Are you ready? If not, repeat the following prayers over yourself until you are.

Prayers of Affirmation

Adonai, Today I receive Your refiner's fire. Your plans for me are good. You discipline me because of Your great love for me.
   Scripture Reference: Jeremiah 29:11, Hebrews 12:6

Adonai, In Your great love for me, run me through Your paces today. You are in the process of conforming me to the image of Your Son, Jesus. Let me stand firm there, Adonai.
   Scripture Reference: Romans 8:29, Ephesians 6:13

Adonai, You don't tarry. Your plans are secure. I choose to stand firm in them today, not drawing back, but believing in Your good works for my life. I will not cast away my confidence in the work you are doing, because it has great reward. I will endure there in order to receive Your promise.
   Scripture Reference: Hebrews 10:35-39

Come Up Higher Questions

1) Lord, would You give me an opportunity to apply the knowledge of this name in my life today?

2) Lord, can You show me what You see in my applying this name today?

3) Lord, can You show me the treasure that You have placed in this person / situation in which I will be applying this name today?

4) What lies have I believed here that I need to break agreement with today in regard to this name/person/situation?

5) What truths do I need to replace those lies with?

Today's Scripture Reference

"But prove yourselves doers of the word, and not merely hearers who delude themselves. For if anyone is a hearer of the word and not a doer, he is like a man who looks at his natural face in a mirror; for once he has looked at himself and gone away, he has immediately forgotten what kind of person he was. But one who looks intently at the perfect law, and law of liberty, and abides by it, not having become a forgetful hearer but an effectual doer, this man will be blessed in what he does."
—James 1:22–25 NASB

Adonai

Stoke the Furnace

Draw What's on Your Heart

Day Three

Know When to Fold 'Em

IT'S FUNNY ALL THIS "love as I love" stuff.

When Jesus says to do that, He means, "Hey, follow Me. Do like I do!"

What I love about Jesus is that He's clear, direct, and a great respecter of people.

That is kind! That IS loving well!

So in Matthew 19 when the Rich Young Ruler decides he'd like to add "Jesus Follower" to his resume, the young man approaches Jesus.

I'm pretty sure he was accustomed to getting what he wanted. Resources typically ensure that.

See here's the beautiful thing about Jesus . . . He sees past the checkbook straight into the heart of the matter. Jesus need pander to no man. Nor is Jesus a punch puller.

Because Jesus doesn't need the money of any rich young ruler, it's already His. All Jesus is doing here is revealing the young man's inability to part with the very resources Jesus entrusted the rich young ruler with in the first place.

So Jesus quickly gets down to the issue.

Telling him to go sell everything he has and come follow Him.

"No can do!" is the Ruler's response.

Here's the interesting part . . . the text tells us Jesus loved the man. It actually grieved Jesus deeply that the man didn't love Him back . . . I'm sure he could give lip service, but the money stood between the two of them.

Note what happens next. When Jesus loves well . . . perfectly actually, Jesus leaves him there. To love his money.

Jesus doesn't beg.

Jesus doesn't start a negotiation, "Okay, how about leaving half your money behind?"

Jesus doesn't say, "Never mind just come along. Somehow we'll make it work."

Jesus doesn't do any of that in His love for this man.

He simply respects the man's "No." Then He leaves him there to love his money.

That's how Jesus loves perfectly.

Get it?

Beloved, here's my prayer for us today. That we learn to see the heart of the issue. That we see past the words being spoken that say, "I love you, I want to come along on this journey of life with you."

When really the answer is, "But I love this thing over here more."

That we discern wisely in this love thing.

That we have the courage to speak to the heart of the matter.

And even more courage to love well, respect the, "No, I can't let this go."

Finally, we are so confident in our mission that we can walk away.

Because sometimes, that's what perfect love looks like.

Ask the Master.

Are you ready to love well today? If not, pray these prayers over yourself until you are.

Prayers of Affirmation

Adonai, Today and moving forward, I choose to believe all that I am and have belongs to You and vice versa. This is the model of Your relationship with Your Father in heaven. This is how I want to live my life in You.

Scripture Reference: John 17:10

Adonai, There is no greater love than the one You demonstrated towards me when You laid down Your life for me. Today I give You my life. All that is in it. I open it all to You, holding nothing back. I submit to Your design for me.

Scripture Reference: John 15:13

Adonai, Thank you for the opportunity to partner with You. That You made us and desire for us to live this way. Today I choose to serve well the plans of the Master.

Scripture Reference: Matthew 20:26-28

Come Up Higher Questions

1) How do I love You in truth today, Lord, in regard to this name?

2) Ask God if He can show you how to love yourself the way He loves you specifically in regard to this name.

3) In what tangible ways can I partner with this name of God to manifest Your presence more clearly in my daily life today, Lord?

4) What gift or talent (equipment or fruit of the Spirit) do I need to manifest this name of Yours on earth today, Lord?

5) Lord, is there anything more You would like to reveal to me about this name?

Today's Scripture Reference

"For the testimony of Jesus is the spirit of prophecy."
—Revelation 19:10b NASB

"But the fruit of the Spirit is love, joy, peace, patience, kindness, goodness, faithfulness, gentleness, self-control; against such things there is no law."
—Galatians 5:22-23 NASB

Adonai

KNOW WHEN TO FOLD 'EM

Draw What's on Your Heart

Day Four

The Master's Key

Have you ever been locked out of a place . . . several keys to flip through . . . all for the same place, but there's only one you need to get you inside to the place where all the other keys will be useful?

Adonai – The Lord.

That key . . . that name . . . is the name that unlocks all His other names in our heart's home.

Little Disclaimer here. It is important we get this right, because we may be able to say the words, "Lord, Lord" with our lips but have our hearts far from Him. (Matthew 7:21–23 NASB, Luke 6:46 NASB). To them He says, "I never knew you, depart from Me you who practice lawlessness." or "Why do you call Me, 'Lord, Lord', but do not do what I say?"

See the importance? If our lips are moving with that name, our knees must bend in obedience to His will. Then, Adonai opens the doors to all of His other names for us to live in the fullness of them.

Adonai. When we call Him by that name, then this is who we are to Him . . .

"They looked to Him and were radiant and their faces will never be ashamed." —Psalm 34:5 NASB

Are you ready for full surrender? If not, pray these prayers over yourself until you can say that you are.

Prayers of Affirmation

Lord, I am led in pathways of life to Your presence, where there is fullness of joy and treasures forevermore.
Scripture Reference: Psalm 16:11

Lord, I am safe and protected always, by Your watchful eye. You lead me in peaceful pathways, tending carefully to make sure I am kept at peace, even in the valleys. You honor me in the presence of my enemies. I am a guest of honor at the table in Your presence. I will dwell with You forever.
Scripture Reference: Psalm 23

Lord, You are with us. You are mighty to save us in times of trouble. I am Your great delight. Lord, You comfort and quiet me with Your love. Lord, You rejoice over me with singing.
Scripture Reference: Zephaniah 3:17

Come Up Higher Questions

1) How can I use this name of God to bring the kingdom of heaven to earth today, Lord?

2) How does this name of God contribute to the flourishing of my neighbors and city, Lord?

3) Lord, can You give me an encouraging word for another regarding this particular name through picture, scripture, song, or word?

4) Ask Him for any further clarification on the above word that He would like to share with you. Write it down. Share these words with that person.

5) Lord, what would You like to say to me today regarding this name that might encourage my own heart? Write it down.

Today's Scripture Reference

"Your kingdom come, Your will be done on earth as it is in heaven."
—Matthew 6:10 NASB

"Behold, I will do something new, now it will spring forth; will you not be aware of it? I will even make a roadway in the wilderness, rivers in the desert."
—Isaiah 43:19 NASB

> "Lord, I want this heart of mine to be Yours. I want to have You settle down here and be perfectly at home. Everything I have belongs to You. Let me show You around."
> —Robert B. Munger, *My Heart Christ's Home*

Adonai

The Master's Key

Draw What's on Your Heart

Day Five

The Holy Hush

We called it the "holy hush." What did we know, we were kids. But I can tell you this, when those eyebrows arched up, eyes big, just the slightest nod of the head pointing down to the direction of her feet . . . the raucous chaos ceased, and you fell in line right under her chin like a soldier.

Here's the thing about Gran . . . Brumma, as I affectionately called her. It was a parental maneuver of epic proportion.

When she was about to "discipline" you, in those moments at her feet, she didn't yell. I don't actually ever recall hearing her raise her voice honestly in my life. Her first line of defense was always the "the holy hush." It was brilliant actually.

The more important the message, the quieter she whispered. As in she captured your full attention when you leaned in with your "listening eyes" locked on hers as she bent to your level. I don't remember many of the words, but I can tell you this . . . it was peaceful in that space at her feet.

Gran was the one who taught me this most valuable lesson of parenting. Far more effective than the raised voice was the "holy hush." She would later divulge that one had to be in full rapt attention to take in a whisper rather than cower from a scream. Wow!

I am reminded of her so often in the same raucous chaos that has gripped our nation. I am reminded that I need to find the whisper. Find the sacred space with Adonai, Lord, Master. Grab His gaze and lean in to lock eyes with Him. To listen intently in the silence for the "holy hush."

Yes! An epic parental move from God Himself – the whisper that commands the raucous chaos to cease . . . If I'm listening.

Beloved, that is my prayer for you today. That you would lock eyes and wait in silence to hear the whisper of Adonai. The Lord and Master over it all. Let Him tell you how the peace returns. How to shake the chaos out of your insides – All in the whisper. Inside the "holy hush" of the sacred space where only you and He exist. There. Are you ready? If not, speak these prayers over yourself until you are.

Prayers of Affirmation

Adonai, You are the Lord and Master over the secret and sacred spaces of both my own heart and the loud and raucous world in which we live. Today I will lock eyes with You and listen for the way in which You will lead. Back to the quiet . . . back to You.
Scripture Reference: Psalm 32:8

Adonai, I will not lean on my own understanding, but in all my ways, with full intention, I will acknowledge You so that You can make my paths straight.
Scripture Reference: Proverbs 3:5-6

Adonai, You call us to Yourself with a gentle whisper designed to soothe and quiet our chaos. I will follow where You lead.
Scripture Reference: Hosea 2:14, I Kings 19:12

Come Up Higher Questions

1) Lord, what is the heart of this name of God towards me today?

2) Lord, is there anything else about the heart of this name of God towards me that I need to know or do today?

3) Lord, is there any area in my life in regard to this name in which I am out of obedience or susceptible to sin? Confess that area in the journal space provided.

4) Lord, what is the gift that You desire to give me in place of that area of weakness or disobedience that I can use to build Your kingdom?

5) Lord, what aspect of Your character or nature would You like to show me, in regard to this name, that I have not seen before?

Today's Scripture Reference

"Therefore there is now no condemnation for those who are in Christ Jesus."
—Romans 8:1 NASB

"What then shall we say to these things? If God is for us, who is against us? He who did not spare His own Son, but delivered Him over for us all, how will He not also with Him freely give us all things?"
—Romans 8:31-32 NASB

"If we confess our sins, He is faithful and righteous to forgive us our sins and to cleanse us from all unrighteousness."
—I John 1:9 NASB

Adonai

THE HOLY HUSH

Draw What's on Your Heart

El Elyon

The Most High God

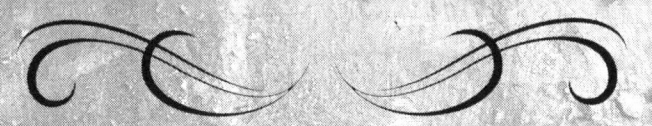

Humbly I kneel to hand You my shame
El Elyon, God Most High,
In one glorious unbecoming
I receive My identity as Your own
The one who breaks through darkness
Has been consecrated to be victorious
Through You, I carry the victory of every battle
This is who You say I am

Today, I believe

Day One

Burn Me Beautiful

My prayer for you today, as I read through Daniel 3, was that the Lord would allow you to walk seeing from the vantage point of the Most High King – El Elyon.

Here's the thing about "The Three Boys" (yes, early teens). They had been discipled in their early years . . . consecrated to their God all their lives.

Make no mistake. Discipleship is not passive parenting. It's proactive training of Frontline Warriors. These were the best youth Israel had to offer . . . offered to El Elyon.

This is the name of God that allows us to be anchored to Him and KNOW that He alone is above all the things, in all the universes . . . of everywhere!

It is this name that helps "The Three Boys" – Shadrach, Meshach, and Abednego, keep their knees stiff when the earthly king of Babylon commands them to bow and worship him.

How many things in our lives are commanding us to bow down and worship them? Our past, our families, our schedules, our jobs, our church (yes, our church), all of our overloaded lives, the issue of the day . . . all commanding our undivided attention.

Who are your little "k" kings? Can we be honest with ourselves? Because we bow our knee somewhere . . . it's either kingdom or culture. If you are coming from a broken background, those knees bow quickly to lots of different things.

"The Three Boys" knew better than to bow to any little "k". They had an internal fire for El Elyon that blazed far brighter than the furnace that was heated to consume them.

Here's the funny thing about the furnace though, even ones that are heated seven times hotter than normal.

When you know El Elyon, you can walk in freedom right into the flames that were designed to consume you . . . because you know that He is waiting for you inside that pit. And to all the onlookers, what they see is El Elyon burning you beautiful. All the dross, all the unnecessary, being consumed as He walks next to you in the flames.

Because what is happening is El Elyon is lighting and stoking the internal flame that burns for Him . . . as the little "k"'s watch outside your furnace door.

In that moment the little "k"'s see El Elyon, and they know who serves whom. And they say His name. They honor your walk into that fiery furnace, and they speak those words that El Elyon longs to hear from each of us, "God Most High, burn me beautiful too."

Are you ready to take that walk? If not, pray these words over yourself until you are.

Prayers of Affirmation

El Elyon, There is no name higher in heaven or on earth than Yours. Today, against culture, I bow my knee to receive Your best for my life. I surrender and submit to the plans that You have for me. For me to live is Christ, and to die is gain.
Scripture Reference: Philippians 2:9, Philippians 1:21

El Elyon, Today I will walk in the freedom that You have died to ensure I received. Whom the Son sets free, is free indeed.
Scripture Reference: John 8:36

El Elyon, I belong to You. You hold my right hand. You guide me with Your counsel, leading me to a glorious destiny. Whom have I in heaven but You? I desire You more than anything on earth. You remain the strength of my heart. You are mine forever.
Scripture Reference: Psalm 73:23–26

Come Up Higher Questions

1) Based on Hebrews 10:35–39, Where have I cast away my confidence in Your name here, Lord?

2) Where am I specifically drawing back in my knowledge of this name, Lord, purposefully not looking at things I need to see? Open my eyes to any blind spots I have to You regarding this name. Confess what He shows you.

3) Where specifically am I in need of endurance regarding this name, Lord?

4) What lies have I been believing about You pertaining to this name, Lord?
   What lies have I been believing about myself pertaining to this name, Lord?
   Confess those lies by writing them down in the journal pages and offer them back to Him.

5) Ask Him what truths He would like to replace those lies with regarding this name. Write those down in the journal pages that follow.

Today's Scripture Reference

"Therefore, do not throw away Your confidence, which has a great reward. For you have need of endurance, so that when you have done the will of God, you may receive what was promised. For yet in a very little while, He who is coming will come, and will not delay. But my righteous one shall live by faith; and if he shrinks back, my soul has no pleasure in him. But we are not of those who shrink back to destruction, but of those who have faith to the preserving of the soul."

—Hebrews 10:35–39 NASB

El Elyon

Burn Me Beautiful

Draw What's on Your Heart

Day Two

True Hope

"I AM "HOPING" HE/SHE/IT WILL CHANGE." I often hear that sentence coming from broken, sobbing women. Sitting in the midst of their heaps of ongoing chaos and destruction.

"Hoping" . . . key word.

The follow-up question is always the same. "What are you anchoring all that "hoping" to?"

It's of utmost importance to know.

Because words matter, so when we are discussing our own futures, and those of our families, we should choose them carefully.

Enter El Elyon – God Most High. In order for radical, sustained life change to occur, this is the only place in which our "hope" can successfully be anchored. Once it's anchored, the work of transformation has the opportunity to begin.

Any other place we drop that "hope" anchor needs to be referred to as "wishing." They are two very different things.

See El Elyon is the One that makes all the difference. He delivers the transformative, DUNIMAS (resurrection) power into our "hoping." While we wait for that transformation, we can intercede on behalf of the thing or person. That's where our DUNIMAS power lies. We may have tried to change the thing, and definitely can't change the person, but we know the One who can. Our job is to battle for the thing or person in the heavenlies.

Proverbs 13:12 tells us that hope deferred makes the heart sick. Want to know why we sit in our chaos and destruction? Because we have literally picked up our "hope" and dropped it at the feet of something inferior . . . not El Elyon. We may place it at the feet of a lot of things . . . fear, unworthiness, knowledge, trying harder, working more, being more patient, waiting, denial. In essence, that is misplaced worship.

These are all inferior covenants, and tantamount to wishing . . . all while the destruction and chaos continues and grows. All while we sit in our excuses.

Beloved! My prayer for you today is this: that you covenant with the hope of El Elyon to be released from whatever chaos or destruction you are battling. That you let go of your inferior covenants and stop wishing.

El Elyon. That name! . . . Are you ready? If not, pray these prayers over yourself until you are.

Prayers of Affirmation

El Elyon, Your name, El Elyon, offers me a secure covenant. It is trustworthy and true, with the power to deliver. It is His name forever. This is His memorial name to all generations.
Scripture Reference: Exodus 3:13-15

El Elyon, You are the source of my hope. You will completely fill me with joy and peace because I trust in You. Then I will overflow with confident hope through the power of the Holy Spirit.
Scripture Reference: Romans 15:13

El Elyon, You have given us Your hope as an anchor for our souls. It is firm and secure – immovable. It is rooted in Your name, Jehovah.
Scripture Reference: Romans 6:19

Come Up Higher Questions

1) Lord, would You give me an opportunity to apply the knowledge of this name in my life today?

2) Lord, can You show me what You see in my applying this name today?

3) Lord, can You show me the treasure that You have placed in this person / situation in which I will be applying this name today?

4) What lies have I believed here that I need to break agreement with today in regard to this name / person / situation?

5) What truths do I need to replace those lies with?

Today's Scripture Reference

"But prove yourselves doers of the word, and not merely hearers who delude themselves. For if anyone is a hearer of the word and not a doer, he is like a man who looks at his natural face in a mirror; for once he has looked at himself and gone away, he has immediately forgotten what kind of person he was. But one who looks intently at the perfect law, and law of liberty, and abides by it, not having become a forgetful hearer but an effectual doer, this man will be blessed in what he does."
—James 1:22–25 NASB

El Elyon

True Hope

Draw What's on Your Heart

Day Three

The Rising Sun

THERE IS SOMETHING ETHEREAL about watching the sun rise over water.

It seems to speak with the voice of God Himself . . . "I am here, just as I promised. I am on time. I am carrying with Me the new mercies that I made just for today. They don't look like yesterday's mercies, and they won't do you any good tomorrow. Today's mercies."

We can set our watches by that same faithfulness. He WILL show up to usher in the light – both literally and figuratively . . . every day. As a matter of fact, the balance of the universe depends on God not being a nanosecond late. Our construct of time depends on the timing of that sunrise. Just as the tides depend on the moon.

All held in that intricately delicate balance by El Elyon Himself – God Most High. Who else could accomplish such a feat uninterrupted from the beginning of time! Imagine someone trying to stop the sunrise. Think about that for a second. It's the exact same thing as someone trying to thwart all that He has planned for you.

El Elyon sits enthroned with everything bowing in submission to Him, and He loves us perfectly. Do you see the endless possibilities of that combination? It starts with love and moves us to big faith. It is what enables us to stand in the middle of the crumbling world and confidently say, "I'm with Him!", no matter what we are seeing happen around us. Ask Joseph. He played the long game in Genesis 45 . . . go check it out. The faithfulness that El Elyon modeled to Joseph, Joseph returned to his brothers against the backdrop of sheer hell.

Beloved, my prayer for you today is this. That you would see the faithfulness of El Elyon. That you would know and BELIEVE that nothing will or can stop Him from getting to you . . . and He WILL be right on time!

Can you trust that? Speak these prayers over yourself until you can.

Prayers of Affirmation

El Elyon, You are God and there is no other.

There is no one like You who can declare the end from the beginning. You declare things not yet completed and say, "My purpose will be established, and I will accomplish all my good pleasure . . . truly I have spoken, truly I will bring it to pass. I have planned it, surely I will do it."
Scripture Reference: Isaiah 46:9-11

El Elyon, if You are for us, who can be against us?
Scripture Reference: Romans 8:31

El Elyon, There is no one that frustrates Your plans. There is no one that can turn back Your outstretched hand.
Scripture Reference: Isaiah 14:24,27

Come Up Higher Questions

1) How do I love You in truth today, Lord, in regard to this name?

2) Ask God if He can show you how to love yourself the way He loves you specifically in regard to this name.

3) In what tangible ways can I partner with this name of God to manifest Your presence more clearly in my daily life today, Lord?

4) What gift or talent (equipment or fruit of the Spirit) do I need to manifest this name of Yours on earth today, Lord?

5) Lord, is there anything more You would like to reveal to me about this name?

Today's Scripture Reference

"For the testimony of Jesus is the spirit of prophecy."
—Revelation 19:10b NASB

"But the fruit of the Spirit is love, joy, peace, patience, kindness, goodness, faithfulness, gentleness, self-control; against such things there is no law."
—Galatians 5:22-23 NASB

> "I believe in Christianity as I believe that the sun has risen: not only because I see it, but because by it I see everything else."
> —C. S. Lewis

El Elyon

The Rising Sun

Draw What's on Your Heart

Day Four

Gran

"I don't have to know all the answers, I just have to know where to find 'em!"

That and oh-so-many others, were gems belonging to my true life's hero, my "Brumma" or "Gran" as we called her . . . My maternal grandmother.

That woman was the epitome of strength to me. She warred in the heavenlies for family generations until Jesus returned, on her knees, travailing in prayer, over her family by the side of her bed. The large Oriental rug, with her knee marks, where the carpet is worn to the backing, still sits anchoring my kitchen table . . . those knee marks firmly planted to the right side of my chair at the head. I couldn't sit down without seeing them. I couldn't get out of that chair without stepping on them. Always reminding me that I had one fierce intercessor railing the heavenlies for my family – every generation until Jesus returns is covered. Many of her prayers yet to be answered.

It was she who showed me El Elyon . . . God Most High. Gran showed me with her unwavering faith. Gran showed me, when in the darkest of childhood days, I would ask her a question about how things would turn out and Gran taught me . . . "Honey, we don't have to know all the answers, we just have to know where to find 'em." Gran stood firm on that foundation of El Elyon when earthly solutions were nigh unto impossible. Gran contended and travailed in the heavenlies for those answers. It was Gran that handed me my fight. It is the richest part of my inheritance from her.

Gran gave me El Elyon. Gran showed me how to travail through the impossible. Most importantly, Gran showed me He always wins . . . by virtue of His position. El Elyon is God Most High. The One with all the answers. Nothing stands against El Elyon, and we are His. That's a combo worth adding to your "believer"!

Beloved, my prayer for you is this, that you know where to go when the answers elude you. That you know that by virtue of your position in Him, you win! Everything you need to know can be found right at the feet of El Elyon.

Today I share my inheritance with you of that precious knowledge that came right from the edges of an old Oriental carpet that anchors a table in the middle of my kitchen. Can you trust Him enough to receive it? It is a sacred trust. If not, repeat these prayers over yourself until you do.

Prayers of Affirmation

El Elyon, I raise You high above all other gods in my life today . . . far above the things that divert my attention from You . . . my "little 'g'" gods. Lord, I ask that You make them fade from me as I turn my full attention and give You my full affection in this moment and every moment from here on out.
Scripture Reference: Psalm 97:9

El Elyon, It is You who possesses all the secrets of the hidden places. It is You to whom an everlasting dominion belongs. It is Your kingdom that endures from generation to generation. You do all according to Your will on both heaven and earth. We cannot stop Your hand, or ask You, "What have You done?" You, El Elyon, do not answer to us.
Scripture Reference: Daniel 4:34-35

El Elyon, It is You who possesses heaven and earth. It is You who sits enthroned above all else. It is You who delivers our enemies into our hands.
Scripture Reference: Genesis 14:17-20

Come Up Higher Questions

1) How can I use this name of God to bring the kingdom of heaven to earth today, Lord?

2) How does this name of God contribute to the flourishing of my neighbors and city, Lord?

3) Lord, can You give me an encouraging word for another regarding this particular name through picture, scripture, song, or word?

4) Ask Him for any further clarification on the above word that He would like to share with you. Write it down. Share these words with that person.

5) Lord, what would You like to say to me today regarding this name that might encourage my own heart? Write it down.

Today's Scripture Reference

"Your kingdom come, Your will be done on earth as it is in heaven."
—Matthew 6:10 NASB

"Behold, I will do something new, now it will spring forth; will you not be aware of it? I will even make a roadway in the wilderness, rivers in the desert."
—Isaiah 43:19 NASB

El Elyon

Gran

Draw What's on Your Heart

Day Five

The Odd Couple

ONE MIGHT HAVE DONE A DOUBLE take on the evening of January 8, 1994, at Washington National's Opera, "Ariadne auf Naxos", had you been fortunate enough to be there in person. You would have had the opportunity to see two best friends having the time of their lives commemorating a shared passion – opera . . . on stage.

The two dear friends, United States Supreme Court Justice Antonin Scalia and the recently passed United States Supreme Court Justice, "Notorious RBG", Ruth Bader Ginsburg, had the opportunity to take their mutually shared love for the opera to the stage together to commemorate the WNO's big love for the both of them. Funny how that worked, right? So far above politics and aisle sides, it would be missing the whole point to go there.

Two fierce opponents by day, arguing from opposite sides of the bench for the liberty and freedom of Americans everywhere. They let that be the minority position in their friendship . . . always. They each espoused such high mutual respect for the worth and value of the other, that they chose to let that guide their relationship. They came together under the core values of liberty and freedom from radically opposing viewpoints. Novel?

Enter El Elyon – God Most High.

While RBG and Scalia held sway in the highest court of our land – El Elyon has been holding court over all of creation from the beginning of time.

My guess is that in His upside-down economy, El Elyon might even cite that famous friendship as a model for how He designed His church to function and model love to the rest of the world. El Elyon's been tirelessly pushing that same agenda since Pentecost.

Everyone is one under Me, El Elyon. My image – Imago Dei – woven into each one of you. Take a look at the lesson of the grafting of the

Gentiles into the church in Ephesians 2. Pretty hard for the Jews to hear that the doors to God Himself were now open to these iconic, cultural, heathenistic outcasts. That was tough. But El Elyon . . . God Most High. The One who sent and sacrificed His own Son to reconcile ALL the "others" to Himself. Who are we, as the created, to question the Creator?

So lest we think this polarization of countrymen is something new, let's think again, Beloved. That, in fact, is my prayer for you. That we would each pin the enemy with the old "RBG / Scalia" maneuver. Reach out to the radically different – the one across the bench, or the aisle. See that difference as a microcosm of who El Elyon created them to be. Mostly see El Elyon and the gifts, talents, and common ground you share. Let that hold the bigger space under the love of El Elyon. The world is watching . . . and waiting. Because one day we are going to be asked to step before El Elyon Himself in tribute to all the overcoming. Are you ready? If not, speak these prayers over yourself until you are.

Prayers of Affirmation

El Elyon, There is no name higher than Yours in heaven or on earth. Lord, let me love well, all the "others" who You Yourself have drawn near to You.
Scripture Reference: Acts 4:12, Ephesians 2:13–14

El Elyon, You have drawn all of us who were once far away to Yourself. You have given us abundant life and liberty. Let us walk that out together, casting aside our differences, in You.
Scripture Reference: Ephesians 2:13–14, John 10:10

El Elyon, You have told us there is no greater love that a man has than he would lay down his life for his friends. Lord, in You we have all been made friends – no differentiation, all heirs of Yours through Jesus, all grafted into the name of El Elyon.
Scripture Reference: John 15:13, Galatians 3:28

Come Up Higher Questions

1) Lord, what is the heart of this name of God towards me today?

2) Lord, is there anything else about the heart of this name of God towards me that I need to know or do today?

3) Lord, is there any area in my life in regard to this name in which I am out of obedience or susceptible to sin? Confess that area in the journal space provided.

4) Lord, what is the gift that You desire to give me in place of that area of weakness or disobedience that I can use to build Your kingdom?

5) Lord, what aspect of Your character or nature would You like to show me, in regard to this name, that I have not seen before?

Today's Scripture Reference

"Therefore there is now no condemnation for those who are in Christ Jesus."
—Romans 8:1 NASB

"What then shall we say to these things? If God is for us, who is against us? He who did not spare His own Son, but delivered Him over for us all, how will He not also with Him freely give us all things?"
—Romans 8:31-32 NASB

"If we confess our sins, He is faithful and righteous to forgive us our sins and to cleanse us from all unrighteousness."
—I John 1:9 NASB

El Elyon

THE ODD COUPLE

Draw What's on Your Heart

El Roi

The God Who Sees

Humbly I kneel to receive from You
El Roi, the promise that I am seen
I am acknowledged
I am welcomed at Your table
I am honored
I have a voice that is valued
I am heard

I am loved by The God Who Sees

Day One

Come Higher

Do you know how much God desires to give you the wisdom and treasures of profound and hidden things? The Bible tells us that, "It is God's privilege to conceal things and the king's privilege to discover them."(Proverbs 25:2 NLT) This has been a tough season for many – 2020! Wow! Who could have fathomed?

El Roi – The God Who Sees.

El Roi would move us out of the darkness of those days in which we have been immersed, and into the light that dwells with Him. El Roi hides nothing FROM us, Beloved. El Roi only hides things FOR us! El Roi brings us on a grand and glorious treasure hunt for the wisdom of Himself as we press in to seek Him and uncover His unshakeable truths.

In the midst of it all, we have the ability to draw close in surrender to Him today. We can learn El Roi in new and deeper ways as He pours out an extra portion of His Spirit on us, bringing revelation. As El Roi shines light into the hidden places, El Roi also releases courage for us to act upon the very things He reveals.

El Roi is inviting each of us to "Come higher in Me, let me teach you how to see what I see with My eyes!"

My prayer for you today, Beloved, is that you will take El Roi up on His invitation to "come higher" in Him. That you will search out the deepest treasures of Himself that will keep you far above the fray of whatever tough season seeks to drag you under.

Are you ready? If not, pray these prayers over yourself until you are.

El Roi

Prayers of Affirmation

El Roi, It is You who changes the times and the epochs. You remove kings and establish kings. You give wisdom to wise men, and knowledge to men of understanding. Today, I choose to believe this very word. I receive the wisdom and knowledge that You delight to share with me.
Scripture Reference: Daniel 2:21

El Roi, It is You who reveals the profound and hidden things. You know what is in the darkness, and the light dwells with You. Lord, I desire to come higher today . . . to live above the fray with You in the heavenlies.
Scripture Reference: Daniel 2:22

El Roi, Today I take my seat with You in the heavenlies. The one next to Him that Christ secured through His sacrifice on the cross on my behalf. This seat enables us to experience the incomparable riches of His grace. Thank you, El Roi, that before the beginning of time, You had figured a way for us to live above the chaos of our earthly home.
Scripture Reference: Ephesians 2:6–7

Come Up Higher Questions

1) Based on Hebrews 10:35–39, Where have I cast away my confidence in Your name here, Lord?

2) Where am I specifically drawing back in my knowledge of this name, Lord, purposefully not looking at things I need to see? Open my eyes to any blind spots I have to You regarding this name. Confess what He shows you.

3) Where specifically am I in need of endurance regarding this name, Lord?

4) What lies have I been believing about You pertaining to this name, Lord?

   What lies have I been believing about myself pertaining to this name, Lord?

   Confess those lies by writing them down in the journal pages and offer them back to Him.

5) Ask Him what truths He would like to replace those lies with regarding this name. Write those down in the journal pages that follow.

Today's Scripture Reference

"Therefore, do not throw away Your confidence, which has a great reward. For you have need of endurance, so that when you have done the will of God, you may receive what was promised. For yet in a very little while, He who is coming will come, and will not delay. But my righteous one shall live by faith; and if he shrinks back, my soul has no pleasure in him. But we are not of those who shrink back to destruction, but of those who have faith to the preserving of the soul."

—Hebrews 10:35–39 NASB

> "Lord, I desire to come higher today . . . to live above the fray with You in the heavenlies."
> —Dawn E. Stephenson, *Who Do You Say I Am?*

El Roi

Draw What's on Your Heart

Day Two

Tilt-A-Whirl

IF YOU'VE BEEN AROUND THE SUN this past year, you know that the world seems like it is tilted on its axis . . . statues are tumbling, voices shout for our attention, whose lives actually matter? What is a "trusted news source" these days?

El Roi – You see, You know . . . You alone are safe to trust.

Lord, May we as Your children learn to tune our voice to YOUR ear. The throne from which all wisdom, revelation, and knowledge flows. It is always a safe place to land, and we are always welcome to boldly approach that throne. It is from that throne You whisper to us the way forward.

Lord! As Isaiah prayed, so do we . . . "He awakens my ear TO LISTEN as a disciple. The Lord has OPENED MY EAR." (emphasis mine).

Beloved, like Isaiah, in this season, it is my prayer that we can echo Isaiah's words back to El Roi. He sees, He knows, He is safe to trust! For truly, these are the only words El Roi longs to hear from us in our chaos . . .

Isaiah 50:4–5 NASB "The Lord God has given Me the tongue of disciples, that I may know how to sustain the weary one with a word. He awakens me morning by morning, He awakens my ear to listen as a disciple. The Lord God has opened my ear; and I was not disobedient nor did I turn back.

Are you ready? If not, repeat these prayers over yourself until you are.

Prayers of Affirmation

El Roi, Find me faithful. Let me overcome by the blood of the Lamb, the word of my testimony, and because I did not shrink back even to the point of death.
Scripture Reference: Revelation 12:11

El Roi, In the middle of the noise, amidst all the indecision, I know I am not lost on Your watch. Hold me close to Your heart. I know that You will never leave me or forsake me.
Scripture Reference: Isaiah 40:11, Deuteronomy 31:6

El Roi, You have been to this place before. You know how it goes. I choose to stand in faith with You today. You have gone before me. You will be with me, and I will not fail.
Scripture Reference: Deuteronomy 31:8

Come Up Higher Questions

1) Lord, would You give me an opportunity to apply the knowledge of this name in my life today?

2) Lord, can You show me what You see in my applying this name today?

3) Lord, can You show me the treasure that You have placed in this person / situation in which I will be applying this name today?

4) What lies have I believed here that I need to break agreement with today in regard to this name / person / situation?

5) What truths do I need to replace those lies with?

Today's Scripture Reference

"But prove yourselves doers of the word, and not merely hearers who delude themselves. For if anyone is a hearer of the word and not a doer, he is like a man who looks at his natural face in a mirror; for once he has looked at himself and gone away, he has immediately forgotten what kind of person he was. But one who looks intently at the perfect law, and law of liberty, and abides by it, not having become a forgetful hearer but an effectual doer, this man will be blessed in what he does."

—James 1:22–25 NASB

"It is from that throne You whisper to us the way forward."
—Dawn E. Stephenson, *Who Do You Say I Am?*

El Roi

Tilt-A-Whirl

Draw What's on Your Heart

Day Three

When the Waves Pound

IN THE HEAT OF IT ALL . . . as the waves pound . . . I want you to write this name down and keep it next to your heart on the hard days. Tuck it in safe and hold it tight.

Beloved, It's my prayer for you today that you say His name, this name, El Roi, over yourself. That you KNOW it as a Memorial Stone in your life, because El Roi has shown Himself to you as "the God who sees" . . . yes, in the darkest of spaces, the most fiery of all the hells.

On one of THOSE days, my prayer is you pull that paper out and call on the name of El Roi.

Perhaps the day started out somewhat "off", which rolled into confusion on all fronts. Kinda felt like the ground around you was anything but firm . . . sound familiar?

You just know, because that urge to move your power nap up to 10:05 a.m. can't be shaken. And you do, because something tells you the day is just getting started.

So you reach out to your prayer partner for support just as the first shot comes across the bow . . . "My father-in-law fell on his boat this weekend and died."

As we roll into the call from one of my own children . . . "I have COVID symptoms." . . . and asthma.

It is in THAT VERY MOMENT, Beloved, that I HAVE GOT TO KNOW I am not crying out to El Roi's back, but rather have locked my eyes onto the eyes of El Roi . . . the God Who Sees.

And I hear El Roi whisper, "This is not unto death, Dear Heart." So I can hold my peace . . . because He IS El Roi. Not only does El Roi see the now, He has already seen the future of the thing.

So Beloved, let El Roi lead you to that table that waits for you in Psalm 23. The one El Roi sets for us in verse 5. Just know this one thing for sure. El Roi will not begin the anointing until the enemies have taken their place there. So tragic death, pull up a chair; COVID symptoms . . . you're on the left. Once you're settled in, El Roi can begin the anointing of MY head with oil. The sign that the honored guest has taken her place . . . watch as she commands all of you to bow to El Roi.

Because, El Roi has seen, you ARE seen in El Roi's line of vision, and El Roi has not lost a battle yet. So take your seat, and call on the name of El Roi.

It is my prayer over you, Beloved, that you let the God Who Sees fight for you, and you will hold your peace. That's a promise. Can you grab hold of that name today?

Are you ready? If not, pray these prayers over yourself until you are.

Prayers of Affirmation

El Roi, I am seeking You with my whole heart. I am standing firm on Your promise that when I do that, You will be found. Find me today, El Roi, the God Who Sees.
Scripture Reference: Jeremiah 29:13

El Roi, You know the way. You make sure my path is safe. Today I stand beside You as we walk beside the still waters. I let You, the God Who Sees, anoint my head with oil in the presence of my enemies . . . because with You, I am safe.
Scripture Reference: Psalm 23

El Roi, You are my front and rear guard. Your eyes see all that needs to be seen to keep me safe in You today. Today, I choose You.
Scripture Reference: Isaiah 52:12

Come Up Higher Questions

1) How do I love You in truth today, Lord, in regard to this name?

2) Ask God if He can show you how to love yourself the way He loves you specifically in regard to this name.

3) In what tangible ways can I partner with this name of God to manifest Your presence more clearly in my daily life today, Lord?

4) What gift or talent (equipment or fruit of the Spirit) do I need to manifest this name of Yours on earth today, Lord?

5) Lord, is there anything more You would like to reveal to me about this name?

Today's Scripture Reference

"For the testimony of Jesus is the spirit of prophecy."
—Revelation 19:10b NASB

"But the fruit of the Spirit is love, joy, peace, patience, kindness, goodness, faithfulness, gentleness, self-control; against such things there is no law."
—Galatians 5:22-23 NASB

El Roi

Draw What's on Your Heart

Day Four

The Righteous Judge

IN A WORLD PLAGUED BY HURT, woundedness, abandonment, rejection, abuse, defiling . . . where does one go to find justice . . . to find healing? To a broken legal system?

Again and again? It seems elusive at best, unfathomable and unattainable at its worst. Who advocates on behalf of those who have been victimized?

El Roi – The God Who Sees . . . that's who!

Many times on my own Journey to Healing, and throughout my life, had I not landed square on the block of El Roi, I would have despaired. There never seemed to be justice or equity.

Until I ran to the arms of El Roi.

There are a few things you need to know today, Beloved, as you walk the path to wholeness. If you take nothing else away today . . . take this!

El Roi sees, El Roi knows, El Roi is safe to trust to make it right.

So today, Beloved, it is my prayer for you that you know you can walk in peace because El Roi is on it. It's what allows us to pray blessings over our enemies and those who hurt us (Matthew 5:54). It's what allows us to roll those huge burdens and injustices back to those on whose shoulders they belong . . . to say, "Mercy first, Lord, but justice!" Knowing that those blessings can include revelation of the wrongs to the wrongdoer. We can let love lead and let the rest go, get on with life, because He's got this! He is El Roi.

In the pit of your hurt, in the hole of your helplessness, can you grab El Roi's promises? Are you ready? If not, repeat these prayers over yourself until you believe them.

Prayers of Affirmation

El Roi, the pillars of Your Throne are righteousness and justice. They co-exist in perfect balance in Your economy. I, therefore, KNOW that all that You've seen of the injustices in my world will be made right and completely whole . . . no matter how badly they've wounded me.
Scripture Reference: Psalm 33:5, Romans 12:9

El Roi, I can rest and release, because I know Your "big guns" are out back to bring restitution and justice to each and every situation. You have fury at the actions of those who hurt what is Yours. Mercy first, but justice.
Scripture Reference: Romans 12:19, Matthew 6:15, 18:35

El Roi, You are a God who sees. You have found me in my wilderness. You have tenderly come to me, to bring restoration. There is not a place where You cannot see me, will not guide me and hold me fast. The darkness is not dark to You, the night shines like day, and darkness is like light to You.
Scripture Reference: Psalm 139, Genesis 16:7–14

Come Up Higher Questions

1) How can I use this name of God to bring the kingdom of heaven to earth today, Lord?

2) How does this name of God contribute to the flourishing of my neighbors and city, Lord?

3) Lord, can You give me an encouraging word for another regarding this particular name through picture, scripture, song, or word?

4) Ask Him for any further clarification on the above word that He would like to share with you. Write it down. Share these words with that person.

5) Lord, what would You like to say to me today regarding this name that might encourage my own heart? Write it down.

Today's Scripture Reference

"Your kingdom come, Your will be done on earth as it is in heaven."
—Matthew 6:10 NASB

"Behold, I will do something new, now it will spring forth; will you not be aware of it? I will even make a roadway in the wilderness, rivers in the desert."
—Isaiah 43:19 NASB

> "El Roi sees, El Roi knows,
> El Roi is safe to trust to make it right."
> —Dawn E. Stephenson, *Who Do You Say I Am?*

El Roi

The Righteous Judge

Draw What's on Your Heart

Day Five

9/11

The phone rang a little after 9 a.m. that morning. Just rolling into the rhythm of math – four grades going strong. Something said, "Pick it up." So I did.

It was my husband. "What's up? I'm in the middle of math." . . . Don't lose the rhythm.

"I just saw a plane fly into the World Trade Center." Plane One. Those were the first words I heard. An uncharacteristically shaken voice.

Well . . . here's what I knew. I knew that he wasn't mistaken. You see, the only thing that stood between his panoramic office window in our trucking terminal in NJ and those two towers was the mile-wide stretch of the Hudson River. Unobstructed view on a clear day. Those towers were the focal point of that window.

Here's where we need to understand the difference between reality and our perception of it. "I'm sure it will be fine." I said, quickly envisioning a small prop plane clipping one of the aerial antennas that rose from the top of those towers.

You see our perception of reality is typically formed by either our experience or frame of reference. Mine was way off base in that moment.

Enter El Roi for a reality check. It came in the voice on the other end of the phone.

"No, this was a big plane. Like a jet carrying people. It flew INTO the building."

I was set straight, but still unprepared.

We would talk for a minute or two more, then hang up.

Until the phone rang again a short bit later. No question, I was picking up.

"Dawn, something's wrong . . . I just saw another plane fly into the second tower. Quick. Turn on the TV!" The phone went dead. It was the last I would hear from or see him for three days. All phone lines were dead.

I remember telling our four children about El Roi – that He saw Daddy, that Daddy wasn't lost, that El Roi knew exactly where Daddy was. Daddy wasn't missing to El Roi. Same with all the daddies in our neighborhood – many who worked in those towers. Our home became a mini-church. Many of those moms, whose husbands were at work in the city . . . in the towers, came over to our home, to cry, to not be alone, to pray. Most of them were not believers.

I told them the same story. El Roi!

El Roi sees them. El Roi knows where they are. Your husbands are not lost, they have never dropped off El Roi's radar.

In the days following, one by one the dads returned home. There were lots of stories of escaping the rubble, the miraculous ways the Lord brought them home in the middle of chaos. But no sweeter story than that of the faithfulness of El Roi.

We all have a story of that day, Beloved. Today, my prayer for you is that you KNOW in your knower . . . more importantly, that you believe in your believer the following: in the unwavering, infallible vision capabilities of El Roi. That El Roi sees you. El Roi CANNOT lose sight of you. El Roi WILL not – even in the middle of the worst crises. El Roi loves us too much.

Do you know that about El Roi? More importantly, do you believe that about El Roi?

Are you ready to believe? Pray these words below over yourself until you are:

Prayers of Affirmation

El Roi, I know that Your eyes roam the earth looking for those who are faithful to You so You can show Yourself strong to them. Lord, find me faithful.

Scripture Reference: II Chronicles 16:9

El Roi, Your eye sees even the sparrow when it falls. You care for its needs. Thank you for valuing us far above sparrows.
Scripture Reference: Luke 12:6

El Roi, It is You that has gone out of Your way to find Hagar in the desert, the woman at the well, the widow burying her only son. Because You saw them, You felt their pain. You cared too much to leave them alone in the middle of it. Thank you for seeing us always, but especially in the middle of our pain.
Scripture Reference: Genesis 16, John 4, Luke 7

Come Up Higher Questions

1) Lord, what is the heart of this name of God towards me today?

2) Lord, is there anything else about the heart of this name of God towards me that I need to know or do today?

3) Lord, is there any area in my life in regard to this name in which I am out of obedience or susceptible to sin? Confess that area in the journal space provided.

4) Lord, what is the gift that You desire to give me in place of that area of weakness or disobedience that I can use to build Your kingdom?

5) Lord, what aspect of Your character or nature would You like to show me, in regard to this name, that I have not seen before?

Today's Scripture Reference

"Therefore there is now no condemnation for those who are in Christ Jesus."

—Romans 8:1 NASB

"What then shall we say to these things? If God is for us, who is against us? He who did not spare His own Son, but delivered Him over for us all, how will He not also with Him freely give us all things?"

—Romans 8:31-32 NASB

"If we confess our sins, He is faithful and righteous to forgive us our sins and to cleanse us from all unrighteousness."

—I John 1:9 NASB

_____

_____

_____

_____

_____

_____

_____

_____

_____

9/11

Draw What's on Your Heart

El Shaddai

The Mighty, All-Sufficient One

Humbly I kneel in the presence of
El Shaddai
Mighty and All Sufficient
To receive my belovedness
From the One who anoints me with
His lavish grace

Day One

Meals on Wheels

IS IT NOT THE MOST PRECIOUS THING to watch a baby suckle at its mother's breast? To watch the actual gift of "life" and sustenance pass from one being to another. Nothing soothes either faster – to be the gifted or the giver.

In Hebrew, El – meaning "mighty" and Shad – having a meaning of "breasted" or "pourer forth" . . . as of blessings in both the physical and spiritual dimensions. In that space, we find that El Shaddai is All-Sufficient to do just that.

El Shaddai doesn't need our cooperation. El Shaddai desires and loves to work with and through us.

Let's take a look at how that works . . . Have you ever been in a situation where you were called on to right the wrong of another? To cover the transgression of those who had acted foolishly . . . sinfully? Perhaps the transgression was yours and someone had to cover that for you.

Regardless . . . I Samuel 25 gives us the details of Abigail. She was an intelligent, beautiful woman. Yet somehow she had managed to marry a prideful, arrogant, very successful businessman – Nabal. Can you imagine her life was "hell in a palace"? You can read about it there.

But here's the short story. King David (yet to be enthroned) had been in hiding with his "band of brothers" in the wilderness of Paran – by Nabal's flocks.

Doing what shepherds do . . . helping Nabal's shepherds guard his flocks. On the run, David goes to inquire about provision for his men from Nabal (whose name means "fool"), in exchange for the work they had been doing alongside Nabal's own shepherds. Nabal rudely dismisses David with nothing provided. David, in a moment of anger, promises to destroy Nabal's household and all that is in it . . . that would have included Abigail.

BUT for the messenger who alerts Abigail (note to self: God ALWAYS provides a pathway for His Beloveds).

Enter El Shaddai – The All-Sufficient One. The Master Creator of the signature move dubbed, "The Suddenlies." When things start flying at breakneck speed, look up. Fix your gaze high. It typically means El Shaddai is unfolding a shift of things.

Like Abigail, El Shaddai invites us into His doings.

The chapter tells us, Abigail quickly gets her equivalent of Uber Eats (her servants) to head down the hill with a full-blown feast to intercept David who is on his way to kill them all. She rides down the backside of the mountain after the feast arrives to meet the whole party . . . and begins to clean up the mess of Nabal. Without Nabal's permission to do any of it (which would have been a mighty risky move to make in that culture). She is a peacemaker in the truest sense of the word.

But Abigail was on a mission ordained by El Shaddai. All had been provided – the revelation of the issue at hand, the bountiful feast was ready and waiting to be served to her family . . . just diverted, and the plan to spare their lives, along with the wisdom and courage to match it.

El Shaddai. The All-Sufficient One.

Everything Abigail needed was in El Shaddai's hand . . . at her disposal. See how He works, Beloved?

The chapter tells us several times "Abigail hurried." Here's the wrap up.

What she did was honor both David and God in her meeting with David. She moved in step with El Shaddai, using the tools of His provision, following His lead, as God moved her out of danger.

And in a quick turn of "The Suddenlies", God honored her. Check it out.

David was thoroughly impressed by her actions. Enough to spare all their lives and marry her! Yes! After God takes Nabal's life within 10 days of that meeting, Abigail finds herself Queen to the Man After God's Own Heart.

This is my prayer for you, Beloved. That you learn to rest in the sufficiency of El Shaddai – that you move in step with Him. That you realize the provision He has placed in your reach to move you out of danger. That you drink from El Shaddai's never-ending fullness. Trust both El Shaddai's plans and El Shaddai's timing. El Shaddai is full of "The Suddenlies" and is excited to invite us into them.

Are you ready? If not, repeat the following prayers over yourself until you are.

Prayers of Affirmation

El Shaddai, You tell us that when we trust in You that we will be like trees planted by the waters that bear continual fruit, never dropping leaves, always blossoming. I receive that from You today. Plant me in Your ever-flowing, never-ending water supply, El Shaddai.
Scripture Reference: Psalm 1:3

El Shaddai, You encompass all that I need. Today I choose to trust in You and lean not on my own understanding. I will acknowledge You as Lord, and I will walk confidently in the straight paths You make for me.
Scripture Reference: Proverbs 3:5–6

El Shaddai, In Your sufficiency You grant me wisdom, and from Your mouth come knowledge and understanding. Today, I receive that wisdom. For it is better to eat a dry crust of bread in peace and quiet than a feast where everyone argues. Today, I choose peace with You.
Scripture Reference: Proverbs 2:6, Proverbs 17:1

Come Up Higher Questions

1) Based on Hebrews 10:35–39, Where have I cast away my confidence in Your name here, Lord?

2) Where am I specifically drawing back in my knowledge of this name, Lord, purposefully not looking at things I need to see? Open my eyes to any blind spots I have to You regarding this name. Confess what He shows you.

3) Where specifically am I in need of endurance regarding this name, Lord?

4) What lies have I been believing about You pertaining to this name, Lord?

   What lies have I been believing about myself pertaining to this name, Lord?

   Confess those lies by writing them down in the journal pages and offer them back to Him.

5) Ask Him what truths He would like to replace those lies with regarding this name. Write those down in the journal pages that follow.

Today's Scripture Reference

"Therefore, do not throw away Your confidence, which has a great reward. For you have need of endurance, so that when you have done the will of God, you may receive what was promised. For yet in a very little while, He who is coming will come, and will not delay. But my righteous one shall live by faith; and if he shrinks back, my soul has no pleasure in him. But we are not of those who shrink back to destruction, but of those who have faith to the preserving of the soul."

—Hebrews 10:35–39 NASB

_____

_____

_____

_____

_____

_____

Meals on Wheels

Draw What's on Your Heart

Day Two

Covenant Love

When we first meet God introducing Himself as El Shaddai, He is working out the details of the Abrahamic Covenant with Abram (soon to be Abraham). You can check it out in Genesis 15 & 17.

Here's the thing you need to know about the Blood Covenant – which the Abrahamic Covenant was. Wellllll . . . they're bloody. In order to fulfill this covenant promise made between two parties – there would need to be a sacrifice – animal sacrifice. So in this particular covenant God requires Abram to kill five assorted animals, cut the three large ones in half – think heifer cow, ram, goat, dove, and pigeon (represents every level of sacrificial offering of His people – richest to poorest). God was making this covenant, ultimately, with ALL of His people, starting with Abram. That's a lot of blood. Abram was to arrange the three large animal halves in two rows, and the two small birds one on each side. The blood would then run down the middle of this atypical aisle.

What happens next is the two parties making the covenant would walk down the aisle, through the blood, together, holding hands. It would seal their covenant – the blood meaning if anything comes between you and I and this agreement, may the same happen to us as these animals. Do you think God is a visual God? Wow! Culturally, this was how it was done.

God promised Abram three things: heirs, land, and blessing. What a covenant. It would be quite an accomplishment because at age 99 Abram was childless and God was uprooting him and his family, to receive a blessing the magnitude of which Abram had no idea.

Lots of backstory here, but it's important.

Here's what we need to know. When the time had come to walk through that aisle of bloodbath, instead of taking Abram's hand and setting off, God puts Abram into a deep sleep and proceeds to show us El

Shaddai – The Self-Sufficient One. God moves down the aisle alone. See the meaning?

El Shaddai... The Self-Sufficient One doesn't "need" us to fulfill His covenant to us. El Shaddai is perfectly capable of fulfilling it on His own. El Shaddai holds EVERY PROVISION AND POWER needed to bring His promise to pass... El Shaddai alone holds it all. The power to fulfill it... HIS! All the provision needed... locked in His storehouses to be released at El Shaddai's command.

But what about Abram? Good question. God desired to birth and deliver those promises to His people THROUGH Abram. However, El Shaddai didn't NEED Abram, El Shaddai wanted Abram! El Shaddai loved Abram. Just like El Shaddai loves us. El Shaddai wants us to partner with Him to deliver the good news of His promises to others. Can you see it?

Beloved, my prayer for you is that you would know El Shaddai. That your partnership with El Shaddai (thankfully under the new covenant of Jesus' death on the cross) would allow you to bask in His sufficiency. We are sufficient through the power of His blood. That blood covers every sin and all the shame attached to them. We are then free to abide in El Shaddai's fulfillment of His unfailing love and provision towards us. The love and provision that allows us to run to El Shaddai as our unfailing Strong Tower. To "rest" like Abram in El Shaddai's completed work.

Can you see it? I pray you can. Recite these prayers over yourself until you do.

Prayers of Affirmation

Lord God, I am equipped with every good thing necessary to do Your will through the blood of Your eternal covenant. I lack NOTHING as I operate in Your will, as You are El Shaddai.
Scripture Reference: Hebrews 13:20–21

Jesus, I thank you for mediating a superior covenant, which is established on better promises. I stand firmly with You to receive those promises, knowing You are faithful.
Scripture Reference: Hebrews 8:6

Thank you, Jesus, that this new covenant contains Your own blood which was poured out for me. That this covenant of peace will not be shaken nor removed because of Your great love and compassion towards us.

Scripture Reference: Luke 22:20 & Isaiah 54:10

Come Up Higher Questions

1) Lord, would You give me an opportunity to apply the knowledge of this name in my life today?

2) Lord, can You show me what You see in my applying this name today?

3) Lord, can You show me the treasure that You have placed in this person / situation in which I will be applying this name today?

4) What lies have I believed here that I need to break agreement with today in regard to this name / person / situation?

5) What truths do I need to replace those lies with?

Today's Scripture Reference

"But prove yourselves doers of the word, and not merely hearers who delude themselves. For if anyone is a hearer of the word and not a doer, he is like a man who looks at his natural face in a mirror; for once he has looked at himself and gone away, he has immediately forgotten what kind of person he was. But one who looks intently at the perfect law, and law of liberty, and abides by it, not having become a forgetful hearer but an effectual doer, this man will be blessed in what he does."

—James 1:22–25 NASB

El Shaddai

Covenant Love

Draw What's on Your Heart

Day Three

Our "More Than Enoughness"

"You won't be able to do that!"

"Who do you think you are to try this?"

"No chance!"

Have those tapes ever played in your mind? Sometimes, perhaps on a continuous loop?

Here's the truth . . . words hurt. Especially those words . . . untrue words. They attack our "more-than-enoughness." They are NOT the truth. They are lies that the enemy fed you through the mouth of another speaking out of their own hurt. For many, they are woven into the very fiber of our stories.

Enter El Shaddai – The All-Sufficient One.

Don't you just LOVE that name?

Whatever you are, don't be neutral on it. We can't afford to be. It's the genesis of our "more-than-enoughness"!

Stick close as we walk it out together. We're about to re-write a story here.

Here's the truth! First, all that God made HE gets to make the declaration over, and your heavenly Father declared you good! From ground zero God looked at Adam and all of creation and declared it good (Genesis 1:31). God saw Adam as so beloved that God did not want to leave Adam alone on the earth. So God made another model to complement /complete him . . . Eve. God loved them so much that He roused from His Throne in heaven to come down daily and walk and talk with them . . . because that's how good and well-loved they were . . . You are. El Shaddai.

When Jesus came again to walk with us, it was the same story, round two. This time, Jesus declares that all that the Father had given to Him, is ours for the asking – such great love – think in the terms of power AND authority. (Luke 10). That's where we win over the enemy . . . with that authority. See El Shaddai's sufficiency here? Ours for the asking. We are sufficient because we are wrapped in El Shaddai – seen as His by God the Father Himself.

That should settle the issue of our "more than enoughness" for us. That should silence the lies that came to us from the stories of another. But just in case you need a little "extra." I encourage you to take some time to read through Ephesians 1 today – concentrate on verses 1–10. Focus on the important things that El Shaddai, in His supreme sufficiency, has given you as your inheritance. Words like . . .

BLESSED! with every spiritual blessing from heaven itself.
CHOSEN! Beloved, you were chosen by El Shaddai. Think about that and how that cancels those horrible tapes that tend to play on the dark days.
DESTINED! For great things because of El Shaddai's sufficiency.
ADOPTED! Taken from our sad stories into El Shaddai's story that we were designed to live.
REDEEMED! That means El Shaddai "writes over" your old story with His victorious plan . . . no matter your age, no matter your baggage.
LAVISHES! Many have never heard the word used in any "love" story they've been attached to. Beloved, that's about to change! Think of SUPER-SIZED, PERFECT LOVE . . . and then multiply that by infinity.
UNIFIES! all things. That means El Shaddai's in the business of redemption, restoration, and reconciliation . . . from our own messes.

Beloved, my prayer for you today is that you see exactly how LOVED and SUFFICIENT El Shaddai has made you to be. That you rest there. That the next time the enemy begins to push play on those old tapes of "worthless," you push the stop button. You stand and say, "Not today. Go sit down, I'm with El Shaddai!"

Are you ready to repaint the landscape of your mind? Start today by agreeing in prayer with the following.

Prayers of Affirmation

Lord, Today I am choosing to stand wrapped in the "enoughness" of El Shaddai. I am fearfully and wonderfully made. Today I stand before the world radiant and unashamed. Thank you, El Shaddai!
Scripture Reference: Psalm 139:14, Psalm 34:5

Lord, Today I stand fully adorned in Your everlasting love for me. I know that I can do all things through You and the strength I receive from You.
Scripture Reference: Jeremiah 31:3, Philippians 4:13

Lord, Sometimes my belief wavers. Help me to remember that it is the only work You require of us. I am blessed when I don't see, yet choose to believe.
Scripture Reference: John 6:29, John 20:29

Come Up Higher Questions

1) How do I love You in truth today, Lord, in regard to this name?

2) Ask God if He can show you how to love yourself the way He loves you specifically in regard to this name.

3) In what tangible ways can I partner with this name of God to manifest Your presence more clearly in my daily life today, Lord?

4) What gift or talent (equipment or fruit of the Spirit) do I need to manifest this name of Yours on earth today, Lord?

5) Lord, is there anything more You would like to reveal to me about this name?

Today's Scripture Reference

"For the testimony of Jesus is the spirit of prophecy."
—Revelation 19:10b NASB

"But the fruit of the Spirit is love, joy, peace, patience, kindness, goodness, faithfulness, gentleness, self-control; against such things there is no law."
—Galatians 5:22-23 NASB

Our "More Than Enoughness"

Draw What's on Your Heart

Day Four

Cooking with Three-Year Olds

For as long as I can remember, it all began the Thursday before Thanksgiving. The easel would go up in the kitchen with the menu outline displayed item by item, appetizer to dessert. Next to the menu item, a "sign-up line" where one of four names would appear. Technically speaking, I had four sous-chefs who would appear on their day to assist in crafting their dishes. Draft age was three. One quick question . . .

Have you ever cooked a Holiday Dinner with a three-year-old?!? Enter El Shaddai – The All-Sufficient One.

I have come to understand a thing or two from those many years of cooking holiday dinners with my children. The most important lesson was this: when God chooses to partner with us to accomplish something . . . it's a lot like cooking with a three-year-old.

Truth of the matter is this . . . I could get the job done much quicker with infinitely less mess and mistakes . . . IF it was about the job. But the more dominant truth of the matter is, I want to involve them in the process, to disciple them, to train and teach them my ways and recipes, some passed from generations. The goal was "to train them up in the way they should go" as Proverbs 22:6 puts it. I loved being with them and watching them master a thing, to have time to study them and get to know how they think and work. Time spent together . . . because I LOVE them. That's what it was about – playing the long game. I certainly was quite capable of putting it all together myself, but there was a bigger picture.

I'm sure that is how El Shaddai thinks about us. El Shaddai doesn't NEED us to accomplish all of His plans in this world, but El Shaddai DELIGHTS in working with us, in spending time with us, in cultivating and growing our gifts, talents, and abilities. The very ones that El Shaddai placed in us before we were born. I can't help but think we must be like three-year-olds in the kitchen to Him. I chuckle every time I read about Jesus in the gospels on mission with the apostles. All the times Jesus takes off for the mountains, or removes Himself from the crowd to separate Himself from them. A genius move on Jesus' part. How else do you remain sinless (smile)?

When I flip the script, I think about what a privilege it is that El Shaddai, the All-Sufficient God, would CHOOSE us "three-year-olds" to play such integral roles in His plans. However, in His All-Sufficiency, El Shaddai is able to complete the good works He began as we yield and allow Him to work through us . . . all part of His self-sufficiency.

Beloved, my prayer for you is that you would yield to the hand of El Shaddai so that He can accomplish all of His good works through you today. That you can understand the height and depth and breadth of El Shaddai's passion for you, His very own three-year-old. (Ephesians 3:18) If you can't, pray these words over yourself until you do.

Prayers of Affirmation

El Shaddai, Thank you for loving me with an everlasting love. Thank you for making me not only Your child, but a joint-heir with Christ that has all of the power and authority that was bestowed upon Him.
Scripture Reference: Jeremiah 31:3, Romans 8:17

El Shaddai, Thank you that You gently lead, teach, guide me into Your ways. That You patiently love and teach me.
Scripture Reference: Isaiah 40:11

El Shaddai, Thank you for being my gentle shepherd, my Kinsman Redeemer, for providing for me always.
Scripture Reference: Psalm 23, Ruth 4:1-10

Come Up Higher Questions

1) How can I use this name of God to bring the kingdom of heaven to earth today, Lord?

2) How does this name of God contribute to the flourishing of my neighbors and city, Lord?

3) Lord, can You give me an encouraging word for another regarding this particular name through picture, scripture, song, or word?

4) Ask Him for any further clarification on the above word that He would like to share with you. Write it down. Share these words with that person.

5) Lord, what would You like to say to me today regarding this name that might encourage my own heart? Write it down.

Today's Scripture Reference

"Your kingdom come, Your will be done on earth as it is in heaven."
—Matthew 6:10 NASB

"Behold, I will do something new, now it will spring forth; will you not be aware of it? I will even make a roadway in the wilderness, rivers in the desert."
—Isaiah 43:19 NASB

El Shaddai

Draw What's on Your Heart

Day Five

Homeward Bound

IF YOU'VE EVER KNOWN A REAL LIFE prodigal child story (or were one), you'd understand the run.

From the porch of the house, to see your child's once-lost silhouette breaking the horizon in the distance . . . I don't think not running would be an option, do you?

Thus was the day, long ago, back in Luke 15:11–32. A day to run, for a father who had never given up his faith-infused hope. Except for one odd fact. His running . . . the "running" of any patriarch would have been culturally taboo in that ancient society. As in, dads don't tuck in their tunics and take off! Try to envision Queen Elizabeth pumping a septic tank! It would have been considered an extremely undignified act.

Enter El Shaddai – The All-Sufficient One.

El Shaddai has the capacity, in His sufficiency, to override cultural taboos and undignified acts (even our own). In fact, the father's running would have been a deflection from the returning son for any who were watching as Dad honored the dishonorable. A kind gesture that would have diverted judging eyes long enough to get the errant son back into the house, put a ring on his finger, and sandals on his feet, while the servants killed and cooked the fatted calf. Quite the welcome for a sin-soaked son. Perhaps the story is familiar from your own life.

But here's the thing about El Shaddai. The sufficiency for all that situation demanded is contained right in that name. The ability to absorb the shame, forgive the offense, to cleanse the slate, to welcome back, to redeem, to restore – all right there, right in that name. El Shaddai – The All-Sufficient One.

Beloved, my prayer for you is that like El Shaddai, we know what to do with all that's wrong. We can take those wrongs of our life and like the son, run towards the arms of an ever-waiting El Shaddai.

That you will find the joy of watching El Shaddai run towards you. So today, I'd ask you, which way are you running? My prayer for you today is that it's towards Him. Are you ready? Pray these prayers over yourself until you are.

Prayers of Affirmation

El Shaddai, You are sufficient. Every sufficiency lies in You and this name. I can never run to a place where I am hidden from Your sight. Help me to turn my run towards Your ever-waiting, faith-fueled, hope-filled arms.
Scripture Reference: Psalm 139:7

El Shaddai, Help me to return to You, to abide in Your sufficiency, to have a broken spirit and a contrite heart, which You do not despise. Lord, keep me holding fast to Your love and justice waiting continually for You. Keep me hungering and thirsting for righteousness.
Scripture Reference: Psalm 51:17, Matthew 5:6, Hosea 12:6

El Shaddai, You tell us if we confess our sins, You remain faithful and just to forgive us those sins and cleanse us from all unrighteousness. Thank you for Your faithfulness to us.
Scripture Reference: I John 1:9

Come Up Higher Questions

1) Lord, what is the heart of this name of God towards me today?

2) Lord, is there anything else about the heart of this name of God towards me that I need to know or do today?

3) Lord, is there any area in my life in regard to this name in which I am out of obedience or susceptible to sin? Confess that area in the journal space provided.

4) Lord, what is the gift that You desire to give me in place of that area of weakness or disobedience that I can use to build Your kingdom?

5) Lord, what aspect of Your character or nature would You like to show me, in regard to this name, that I have not seen before?

Today's Scripture Reference

"Therefore there is now no condemnation for those who are in Christ Jesus."
—Romans 8:1 NASB

"What then shall we say to these things? If God is for us, who is against us? He who did not spare His own Son, but delivered Him over for us all, how will He not also with Him freely give us all things?"
—Romans 8:31–32 NASB

"If we confess our sins, He is faithful and righteous to forgive us our sins and to cleanse us from all unrighteousness."
—I John 1:9 NASB

> "So today, I'd ask you, which way are you running? My prayer for you today is that it's towards Him."
> —Dawn E. Stephenson, *Who Do You Say I Am?*

El Shaddai

HOMEWARD BOUND

Draw What's on Your Heart

Elohim

Supreme or Mighty God, Creator, Relational God

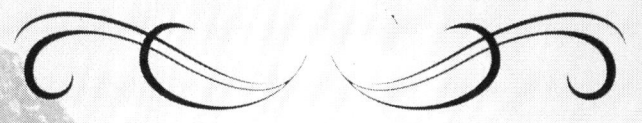

Victoriously I arise, a Valiant Warrior,
O Elohim, Scripter of my story,
To walk in the anointing of words
spoken over me in eternity past

Day One

When Chaos is Called to Order

WHEN THE ROADMAP OF YOUR LIFE looks like it just got shot out of a confetti cannon, with millions of pieces dancing in the air all around you in a blizzard . . .

That's when we call on the name of Elohim – The Creator.

Join me in the very beginning of it all – Genesis 1:1.

It's the name God chooses to introduce Himself to us at the outset of His word . . . CREATOR.

"In the beginning God (Elohim) created." Genesis 1:1 NIV.

As in the One who puts it all together, again and again if need be . . . constantly creating. It was His first order of business. Watch how it works . . .

Genesis 1:2 NASB, "The earth was formless and void, and darkness was over the surface of the deep, and the Spirit of God was moving over the surface of the water."

Can you relate? Do words like "formless" and "void" and "darkness" describe some sector of life right now?

Have they ever? If not, hold on; we all are called to that place in life at one time or another in varied degrees. Right now, if not for yourself, for someone you love.

Perhaps it's all "formless", "void", and "dark". Not only that, but the "darkness was over the surface of the deep" – deep darkness.

Some of us have existed in deep darkness in some areas, or all areas, for a long time. Usually what we find in the deep darkness are the hurts, habits, and hang-ups that have kept us spinning in chaos throughout life.

If it weren't for the last phrase of that verse, it might remain hopeless. So hang on . . . look up, Child!

"And the Spirit of God was moving over the surface of the waters" . . . the deep darkness.

Because Elohim's just getting started. Like an artist beginning to visualize in their mind's eye . . . all the beauty of YOU!

And Elohim gets to work. Speaking, dividing, joining, coloring, adding textures and shapes and good and beautiful and layering it all with gifts and talents . . .

Elohim speaks into the darkness with His voice, and it obeys Elohim's every command. Piece by piece, the darkness disappears – overtaken by light, bright ones and dim ones.

Slowly chaos releases its grip . . . unraveling at warp speed; taking shape at the command of its master.

It won't stop, can't stop until Elohim says the words . . . "It is good!"

Just like Elohim's plans for you in Jeremiah 29:11 NLT, "I know the plans I have for you," says the Lord. "They are plans for good and not for disaster, to give you a future and a hope." This verse takes on significantly greater meaning when we understand it in context. God is speaking this prophecy over His people, Israel, WHILE THEY ARE IN BONDAGE in Babylon!

My prayer for you, Beloved, is that you know Him as Elohim. That you let Him move over the deep darkness, chaos, and bondage of your own life. Let Elohim have at it.

Because Elohim's already told you, chaos, darkness, or bondage have no place there.

Are you ready? If not, pray these words over yourself until you are.

Prayers of Affirmation

Elohim, Today I choose to believe that in You there is no darkness. I thank you that You are the light of the world and no darkness can overcome You.
Scripture Reference: John 8:12, 1 John 1:5

Elohim, As You separated land from sky, earth from water, night from day, so You organize my life. You are a God of order. I surrender my life to You to organize and to call to righteousness and all of the fruit that it bears.
Scripture Reference: Genesis 1, Psalm 1

Elohim, You go before me and follow me. You place Your hand of blessing on my head. Such knowledge is too wonderful for me, too great for me to understand! I can never escape from Your Spirit! I can never get away from Your presence! If I go up to heaven, You are there; if I go down to the grave (in my darkest chaos), You are there . . . even there Your hand guides me, and Your strength supports me. Thank you, Elohim, that in all Your creating, You can never lose sight of me!

Scripture Reference: Psalm 139

Come Up Higher Questions

1) Based on Hebrews 10:35–39, Where have I cast away my confidence in Your name here, Lord?

2) Where am I specifically drawing back in my knowledge of this name, Lord, purposefully not looking at things I need to see? Open my eyes to any blind spots I have to You regarding this name. Confess what He shows you.

3) Where specifically am I in need of endurance regarding this name, Lord?

4) What lies have I been believing about You pertaining to this name, Lord?
   What lies have I been believing about myself pertaining to this name, Lord?
   Confess those lies by writing them down in the journal pages and offer them back to Him.

5) Ask Him what truths He would like to replace those lies with regarding this name. Write those down in the journal pages that follow.

Today's Scripture Reference

"Therefore, do not throw away Your confidence, which has a great reward. For you have need of endurance, so that when you have done the will of God, you may receive what was promised. For yet in a very little while, He who is coming will come, and will not delay. But my righteous one shall live by faith; and if he shrinks back, my soul has no pleasure in him. But we are not of those who shrink back to destruction, but of those who have faith to the preserving of the soul."

—Hebrews 10:35–39 NASB

_____

_____

_____

_____

_____

_____

_____

_____

_____

Draw What's on Your Heart

Day Two

Chipped Away

HAVE YOU EVER NOTICED, chaos is the predecessor of all creation? Prior to the "David", there was a block of marble that sat untouched for over a quarter of a century, through a string of commissioned artists, before a 26-year-old Michelangelo convinced the Commissioners that he should be the one to see this important piece to completion.

Can you think of a time in your own life that chaos ruled in some way, shape, or form? From the littlest of things (a messy drawer or room) to the unimaginable (critical injury of a child, divorce, death of a spouse) . . . something is just hopelessly "out of order"? Can you find a place chaos is ruling now?

Enter Elohim – God the Creator.

From before time began, Beloved, God Himself had cast a vision for you; much like Michelangelo had for the David. Jeremiah 1:5NLT reveals that very precious truth.

"I knew you before I formed you in your mother's womb. Before you were born I set you apart and appointed you as my prophet to the nations."

Elohim has always held His vision for you. He has always simply been waiting for the appropriate moment in the history of the world to drop you into His story.

See, here's the thing about Elohim. Look outside at His creation. It's actually far beyond our comprehension.

Elohim never runs out of ideas on how to take the chaos over and bring it to order . . . according to His design. Elohim begins with the end in mind. Like any good artist, His vision is cast.

Michelangelo, when asked how he came to create the David, replied, "I simply chipped away everything in the marble that was not the David."

Elohim works like that in our chaos. According to His plans for us, Elohim chips . . . saying to Himself, to us, "I know the plans I have for you, plans for good and not for evil; plans to give you a future and a hope." Jeremiah 29:11

While we see a huge mass of marble that had been laying in a yard for years, Elohim has a plan and is hard at work.

Make no mistake, it is us who are shortsighted. Elohim sees the masterpiece of, and in, us. He is chipping and creating. Busy being Elohim! Calling the chaos to order. Have no doubt . . . The One who formed the hands that chipped away at the marble of the David is still creating today, in our lives, if we let Him.

Beloved, it is my prayer for you today that you will hear Elohim's whisper and allow Elohim to begin the process of making roads in the wilderness of your life and rivers in the desert of your heart. Make no mistake, even when you cannot see, Elohim is busy doing the "something new"!

Can you trust Elohim with the mass of marble of your life? Can you submit to His vision? Are you ready?

If not, pray these words over yourself until you are.

Prayers of Affirmation

Elohim, I will not call to mind the former things, or ponder things of the past. Today I will wait in glorious anticipation of the "something new" that You are busy doing! I will wait for it to spring forth; I will be aware of it! Elohim, I look forward to walking every roadway in the wilderness You are now creating, and drinking from all of the rivers in the desert that are even now springing up!

Scripture Reference: Isaiah 43:18–19

Elohim, I am in Christ. I am a new creature, one made by Your design. Today I receive that new creation according to Your design. My old life is gone thanks to Your work on the cross. Glory Up! My new life is here. Today I embrace it and walk fully into it!

Scripture Reference: II Corinthians 5:17

Elohim, From this day forward, in You, I will live and move and have my being. I can do this because I am Your creation . . . Your offspring!

Scripture Reference: Acts 17:28

Come Up Higher Questions

1) Lord, would You give me an opportunity to apply the knowledge of this name in my life today?

2) Lord, can You show me what You see in my applying this name today?

3) Lord, can You show me the treasure that You have placed in this person / situation in which I will be applying this name today?

4) What lies have I believed here that I need to break agreement with today in regard to this name / person / situation?

5) What truths do I need to replace those lies with?

Today's Scripture Reference

"But prove yourselves doers of the word, and not merely hearers who delude themselves. For if anyone is a hearer of the word and not a doer, he is like a man who looks at his natural face in a mirror; for once he has looked at himself and gone away, he has immediately forgotten what kind of person he was. But one who looks intently at the perfect law, and law of liberty, and abides by it, not having become a forgetful hearer but an effectual doer, this man will be blessed in what he does."

—James 1:22–25 NASB

Elohim

Draw What's on Your Heart

Day Three

Sing A New Song

"STOP IMITATING THE IDEALS AND OPINIONS of the culture around you but be inwardly transformed by the Holy Spirit through a total reformation of how you think. This will empower you to discern God's will as you live a beautiful life, satisfying and perfect in His eyes." Romans 12:2 TPT

For today, let's break habit and talk about how I transform who I am (the old me) into who I am in Christ (who I am becoming).

One thing is certain in this crazy culture. We cannot deny the chaos around us, we cannot remain stagnant in it. Our identity in Christ as a new creation is available to us through Him and His work on the cross . . . check it out.

"Therefore if anyone is in Christ, the new creation has come: the old is gone, the new is here!" II Corinthians 5:17 NLT

So we can begin the telling of our new story this way . . .

Speak it over yourself, until you believe it. If the God who created us first spoke it to us, shouldn't we "affirm" what He says about us? After all, we are His design. He has naming rights.

Because here's the truth as Bill Johnson, Pastor of Bethel Church in Redding, CA, so succinctly puts it, "I cannot afford to have a thought in my head that He doesn't think about me." Am I right?

Beloved, THIS is how we align with Elohim. You speak Elohim's truth about you to yourself today. You are beloved and becoming.

It's time to purge the thoughts in our heads that are not Elohim's towards us. Are you ready? If not, say these prayers over yourself until you are.

Prayers of Affirmation

Elohim, You are MY Creator. Before You formed me, You knew me and You set me apart to accomplish all that You have for me according to Your plans for my life. Today I will commit to aligning my thoughts about myself with Yours. Can You please speak Your thoughts about me to me right now?
Scripture Reference: Jeremiah 1:5

Elohim, You hovered over my chaos, ready to create order . . . with a word You speak, with Your pneuma breath You breathe, the darkness becomes light in my world, in my life. The night becomes day, the land appears from the chaos called my Sea of Despair . . . hope returns. You set the stage for me . . . provision for my needs before I've arrived. Grass, trees, vegetation, animals, companions. Lord, You are ever mindful of me and my needs, ever compassionate. Creating order . . . step by step. I am fearfully and wonderfully made.
Scripture Reference: Genesis 2, Psalm 149:13

Elohim, I sin and You've made a way back to You . . . out of Your wild and crazy love for me.
 You continue by making beautiful new paths for me in the midst of the chaos of this crazy world. I can leave the past in the rear view mirror, hand in hand with You. Your Almighty Hand will create roadways in the wilderness, streams in the desert . . . just for me. I've been created to hold a special place in Your heart . . . "I am My Beloved's and My Beloved is mine.", that's the love song You sing over me. I flourish there.
Scripture Reference: John 3:16, Isaiah 43:18–19, Song of Songs 6:3

Come Up Higher Questions

1) How do I love You in truth today, Lord, in regard to this name?

2) Ask God if He can show you how to love yourself the way He loves you specifically in regard to this name.

3) In what tangible ways can I partner with this name of God to manifest Your presence more clearly in my daily life today, Lord?

4) What gift or talent (equipment or fruit of the Spirit) do I need to manifest this name of Yours on earth today, Lord?

5) Lord, is there anything more You would like to reveal to me about this name?

Today's Scripture Reference

"For the testimony of Jesus is the spirit of prophecy."
—Revelation 19:10b NASB

"But the fruit of the Spirit is love, joy, peace, patience, kindness, goodness, faithfulness, gentleness, self-control; against such things there is no law."
—Galatians 5:22–23 NASB

Elohim

Sing A New Song

Draw What's on Your Heart

Day Four

The Skillful Surgeon

The last thing I remember was the needle coming at me and the surgeon's voice saying, "Well this should be the worst part of it for you." An hour later I woke up with two less sheared-off, broken molars in the back of my mouth.

Well all I can say was, "It was time . . . past time actually!" In the process of life's chaos the past few years I had clenched and ground my teeth in my sleep so hard (stress) that I had sheared those teeth clear past the point of repair. Having tried a very brief stint in the general dentist chair for this extraction it became clear that this was a job for the oral surgeon.

As in "Knock me out, and wake me up when it's all over!"

Sometimes life is just like that though, right? Sometimes the wound or repair work needed is so deep that we have to be knocked out to get to the root of the problem.

Enter Elohim – Creator God.

Elohim knows the heart of the matter. In all honesty, Elohim knows the heart of the wound.

Just as the oral surgeon's nurse told me after hearing my encounter at the dentist . . . "Oh yes! That's why we have specialists. We do this all day, every day." Some jobs are just best left to the experts.

Let's head back to Genesis 2:21 NLT. "So the Lord God caused the man to fall into a deep sleep. While the man slept, the Lord God took out one of the man's ribs and closed up its place with flesh."

When God saw the condition of Adam, Elohim said (my paraphrase), "I don't want you to do this life thing alone. That's not how I designed this to work." So God proceeded to knock Adam out. When he woke up, he was minus a rib and up an "Ezer"– a helpmate . . . or a wife (also translated as a warrior, FYI).

That Elohim, He knows what He's doing!

Listen, there's a time when we may need to be "knocked out" by Elohim for a hot second. But I want you to know this. If Elohim takes you down, or knocks you out, it's because of His kindness towards you. It is not for the sole intention of wounding. It is for the intention of "setting things right", according to the design plans of Elohim Himself. Take a look at what Elohim has to say about it all in Isaiah 46:13 NLT.

"I am ready to set things right, not in the distant future, but right now! I am ready to save Jerusalem and show my glory to Israel."

What Elohim's saying is it's time to go under for a minute. I've got work to do to get you to look like the YOU that I've created you to be. Let me operate.

Well, I woke up in that chair down two teeth and with a recovery journey ahead, but I knew this. Long term, no more chance for infection or potential sepsis. The "knocking out" was the laying of the foundation for all the new that eventually will replace all that was taken. I will have permanent new, infallible teeth back there to look forward to – much like life. Eventually when it's all said and done here we will have a whole new infallible body, soul, spirit, and emotions to look forward to.

But first, at some point in life, we are going to have to go under. Beloved, that's my prayer for you is that you submit to the grand and glorious process of Elohim. That you can trust the goodness of Elohim's plans for you. That the "knocking out" won't scare you. That you will know, when it's time, that it is all for your good and for His glory. Are you ready? If not, speak these prayers over yourself until you are.

Prayers of Affirmation

Elohim, I know that the plans You have for me are for good and not for evil. They are to give me a future and a hope. I believe and choose today to trust You, sight unseen, with all my heart and lean not on my own understanding.

Scripture Reference: Jeremiah 29:11, Proverbs 3:5-6

Elohim, You knit me together in my mother's womb. Before I was formed, You knew me. You had a design for my life. Today I choose to trust You with Your plan for my life.
Scripture Reference: Psalm 139:13-14

Elohim, You are worthy, O Lord our God, to receive glory and honor and power. For You created all things, and they exist because You created what You pleased. Thank you, Elohim, that I am pleasing to You."
Scripture Reference: Revelation 4:12

Come Up Higher Questions

1) How can I use this name of God to bring the kingdom of heaven to earth today, Lord?

2) How does this name of God contribute to the flourishing of my neighbors and city, Lord?

3) Lord, can You give me an encouraging word for another regarding this particular name through picture, scripture, song, or word?

4) Ask Him for any further clarification on the above word that He would like to share with you. Write it down. Share these words with that person.

5) Lord, what would You like to say to me today regarding this name that might encourage my own heart? Write it down.

Today's Scripture Reference

"Your kingdom come, Your will be done on earth as it is in heaven."
—Matthew 6:10 NASB

"Behold, I will do something new, now it will spring forth; will you not be aware of it? I will even make a roadway in the wilderness, rivers in the desert."

—Isaiah 43:19 NASB

Draw What's on Your Heart

Day Five

The Odd Couples

I'm sure you've seen them, perhaps even chuckled a time or two. They seem strangely mismatched (usually why they draw my attention initially). They always make me take pause and ignite a fury of imaginary flames . . . stories of my own creation. Of what am I speaking? To whom am I referring? Well, it's the odd couples.

This coupling can occur anywhere and everywhere. Look in nature, it gives us prime examples. Look at that irritant to many, Poison Ivy. Did you know that the cure for Poison Ivy, Virginia Creeper and Jewelweed, are often found in areas where poison ivy grows? They are oftentimes right next to each other! Fascinating! The problem and the cure dwelling harmoniously side by side. What a great love Elohim has for us, not desiring that we should have to search things out. A shower of Elohim's mercy towards us. When we have eyes to see!

Therein is the secret sauce!

Enter Elohim. The Creator God. Elohim's ability to speak to us through nature and how Elohim uses it to mirror what is happening in the spiritual realm never ceases to amaze me. Take, for example, Psalm 65:9–13 TPT.

"Your visitations of glory bless the earth; the rivers of God overflow and enrich it. You paint the wheat fields golden as You provide rich harvests. Every field is watered with the abundance of rain showers soaking the earth and softening its clods, causing seeds to sprout throughout the land. You crown the earth with its yearly harvest, the fruits of Your goodness. Wherever You go, the tracks of Your chariot wheels drip with oil. Luxuriant green pastures boast of Your bounty as You make every hillside blossom with joy. The grazing meadows are covered with flocks, and the fertile valleys are clothed with grain, each one dancing and shouting for joy, creation's celebration! And they're all singing their songs of praise to you!"

The summary of it is this. Nature sings praises to Elohim. The life-sustaining water He provides. The cycle of life in nature itself. The meadows and valleys shout for joy arrayed in their gloriously beautiful splendor.

All there for those who have eyes to see.

Just as Elohim packed nature with gifts of His creativity, so has Elohim packed each and every one of His Image Bearers – us! Imago Dei. We are created in Our Creator's image. The gifts that Elohim has so delightfully placed in each of us bear witness to Elohim's own incredible creativity.

The creativity placed in us by Elohim desires to partner with us to draw others to Himself through us! You may need to read that again. God is a Master Elohim. Elohim's gifts in you, Elohim's plans for you, all designed to be used by you to bring His kingdom to earth. You, Beloved, are a bearer of His image.

A strange partnership, yes. Each of us and Elohim. Yet Elohim delights in these partnerships. They are what draw others to Him – our Imago Dei. Our gloriously, delightful strange partnership with Elohim Himself.

It is my prayer for you today, Beloved, that you would take time to ask Elohim to draw out your giftings. Ask Elohim how He would like you to partner with Him to bring some heaven to earth today.

Are you ready? If not, pray the following over yourselves until you are.

Prayers of Affirmation

Elohim, Today because of Your work, I will live in joy and be led forth in peace. All the mountains and the hills before me will burst into song, and the trees of the field will clap their hands . . . this is for the Lord's renown, for an everlasting sign that will endure forever. Just like our worship of You, Elohim. Thank you for showing us the way through Your creation.
Scripture Reference: Isaiah 55:13

Elohim, Today I will lift my voice in worship, despite what I see around me. You've told us that if we don't worship, You will make the rocks cry out to sing Your praises.
Scripture Reference: Luke 19:40

Elohim, Thank you for being a masterful creator. Thank you for the eternal flow of creativity that You have brilliantly placed around us in this world, and more importantly, each other. Draw me today to partner not only with You with my creativity but, Elohim, draw me to the right others and their creativity to bring Your kingdom to earth.

Scripture Reference: I Corinthians 12:27, Romans 12:5-6

Come Up Higher Questions

1) Lord, what is the heart of this name of God towards me today?

2) Lord, is there anything else about the heart of this name of God towards me that I need to know or do today?

3) Lord, is there any area in my life in regard to this name in which I am out of obedience or susceptible to sin? Confess that area in the journal space provided.

4) Lord, what is the gift that You desire to give me in place of that area of weakness or disobedience that I can use to build Your kingdom?

5) Lord, what aspect of Your character or nature would You like to show me, in regard to this name, that I have not seen before?

Today's Scripture Reference

"Therefore there is now no condemnation for those who are in Christ Jesus." —Romans 8:1 NASB

"What then shall we say to these things? If God is for us, who is against us? He who did not spare His own Son, but delivered Him over for us all, how will He not also with Him freely give us all things?"

—Romans 8:31-32 NASB

"If we confess our sins, He is faithful and righteous to forgive us our sins and to cleanse us from all unrighteousness."

—I John 1:9 NASB

The Odd Couples

Draw What's on Your Heart

Immanuel

God With Us

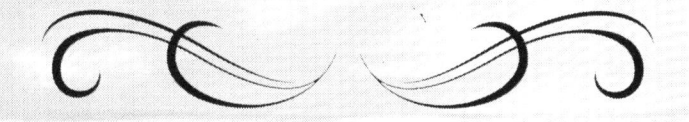

Victoriously I arise,
God with me, in me, for me,
Immanuel
To carry the touch of the Divine

Day One

Loving "Through" The Thing

TODAY I WOKE UP TO THE VERSE that has Immanuel's voice being heard . . . speaking right to us about how Immanuel wants us to love . . . on each other. That would be in John 13:34. Immanuel told them He was about to drop a novel concept in their lap – a new commandment, Immanuel called it. We would be able to bring it to completion because of Immanuel – God with us. It went like this.

"I give you a new commandment: that you should love one another. Just as I have loved you, so you too should love one another." John 13:34 AMPC

Some of us may say, "No new news here . . . we've been hearing that since Moses came down the mountain with the Ten Commandments!"

Well actually, this time there was a twist.

Backtrack to the middle of the verse to find the gold. See it? It's hidden in the words, "Just as I have loved you."

So while the Commandments gave us the written (law) version, Jesus steps in and gives us the human (love-in-action) version. What the Commandments tell us about love, they can't fulfill the duty of showing us. Jesus says it best this way in Matthew 5:17–20 TPT:

"If you think I've come to set aside the law of Moses or the writings of the prophets, you're mistaken. I have come to fulfill and bring to perfection all that has been written. Indeed, I assure you, as long as heaven and earth endure, not even the smallest detail of the law will be done away with until its purpose is complete. So whoever violates even the least important of the commandments, and teaches others to do so, will be the least esteemed in the realm of heaven's kingdom. But whoever obeys them and teaches their truths to others will be greatly esteemed in the realm of heaven's kingdom."

Fulfilling the law of the Commandments is His job. Jesus takes the flatness of the one dimensional tablet's command to love, and He brings it to life by showing us Himself as Immanuel – God with us.

What Immanuel's inviting us to do is "watch Me for the win" on this "LOVE" thing. Do what I do, you can because I'm with you . . . and I'm for you!

Because the important thing to know about Jesus modeling "LOVE" for us to follow, is that it's not just WHAT He does, it's WHO HE IS.

Let that sink in for a second . . .

Immanuel cannot do anything outside of love, because Jesus' name IS His nature.

In Immanuel's perfection, He is incapable of operating contrary to His nature. That would be sin . . . which Jesus is also incapable of.

Today, Beloved, my prayer for you is that you can simply ask yourself this question: How closely is my love for myself, and then for others, matching the way Jesus is inviting us to love? Am I ready to receive that level of strength?

Are you ready to know the love of Jesus? If not, pray these prayers over yourself until you are.

Prayers of Affirmation

Immanuel, Today I am choosing You. I am choosing to open myself up to receive Your love. Then out of that overflow, I can love others as You first loved me. Lord, show me Your love today so I can show it in the same way to others.

Scripture Reference: I John 4:19

Immanuel, Thank you for loving me well. Thank you that I can never fall out of favor with You. Thank you that You have made a way for us to reach You. Lord, today I confess any sin that has remained unconfessed in my life. (Pause here, and ask Him to show you what that is). Thank you that Your love for me allows those sins to be forgiven.

Scripture Reference: I John 1:9

Immanuel, Your love for me is as vast as the oceans. Lord, help me to have the power to understand how wide, how long, how high, and deep Your love is for me.

Scripture Reference: Ephesians 3:18

Come Up Higher Questions

1) Based on Hebrews 10:35–39, Where have I cast away my confidence in Your name here, Lord?

2) Where am I specifically drawing back in my knowledge of this name, Lord, purposefully not looking at things I need to see? Open my eyes to any blind spots I have to You regarding this name. Confess what He shows you.

3) Where specifically am I in need of endurance regarding this name, Lord?

4) What lies have I been believing about You pertaining to this name, Lord?
   What lies have I been believing about myself pertaining to this name, Lord?
   Confess those lies by writing them down in the journal pages and offer them back to Him.

5) Ask Him what truths He would like to replace those lies with regarding this name. Write those down in the journal pages that follow.

Today's Scripture Reference

"Therefore, do not throw away Your confidence, which has a great reward. For you have need of endurance, so that when you have done the will of God, you may receive what was promised. For yet in a very little while, He who is coming will come, and will not delay. But my righteous one shall live by faith; and if he shrinks back, my soul has no pleasure in him. But we are not of those who shrink back to destruction, but of those who have faith to the preserving of the soul."

—Hebrews 10:35–39 NASB

Loving "Through" The Thing

Draw What's on Your Heart

Day Two

Every Day Is Christmas

WE TEND TO ASSOCIATE GOD using this name for Himself at Christmas where we find Him as a King Baby. The setting is not something we would immediately associate as either King or God – meek and lowly, humble and holy, in a stable, poor as dirt.

Isn't it just like God to announce Himself here as Immanuel and then upend our expectations in such radical ways?

Immanuel . . . not only God with us, but God for us, God in us, God through us.

Usually in VERY unexpected ways.
In the furnace . . . Immanuel.
In the addiction unit . . . Immanuel.
In the breast mass . . . Immanuel.
In the miscarriage . . . Immanuel.
In the parenting of littles in COVID . . . Immanuel.
In the losing of a job . . . Immanuel.
In the slipping away of a spouse . . . Immanuel.
Call His name . . . Immanuel.
Remember God's name is His nature.
God acts in accordance with it.

Watch Immanuel show up in such unexpected ways . . . looking like help from the places you least expect.

So many times Immanuel's hands and feet and ears belong to us . . . as in God through us.

We have the honor to deliver Immanuel in the middle of an addiction unit, or sit in someone's furnace with them. Perhaps Immanuel looks like your listening ear as one of His own processes a diagnosis. Bring Immanuel to the mom of littles who is fatigued. Let's cook them dinner or take her kids for the afternoon. Immanuel.

So many assignments await us to bring Immanuel where He is needed.

Beloved, it is my prayer for you today that you see, with Immanuel's eyes, the places He is longing to be taken. That you would obediently bring Him there to others who need a taste of Him today, even if it's uncomfortable. Are you ready? If not, pray these prayers over yourself until you are.

Prayers of Affirmation

Immanuel, Today, I am going to trade my heavy yoke for Yours. I will commit, just for today, to learning from You because Your yoke is easy and Your burden is light.
Scripture Reference: Matthew 11:28–29

Immanuel, You have promised that all of Your children will be taught by You and great will be their peace. Today I open myself to be taught by You.
Scripture Reference: Isaiah 54:13

Immanuel, Today I am going to take You up on Your invitation to come away with You and rest for a while. Today, I am going to abide in You.
Scripture Reference: Mark 6:31

Come Up Higher Questions

1) Lord, would You give me an opportunity to apply the knowledge of this name in my life today?

2) Lord, can You show me what You see in my applying this name today?

3) Lord, can You show me the treasure that You have placed in this person / situation in which I will be applying this name today?

4) What lies have I believed here that I need to break agreement with today in regard to this name / person / situation?

5) What truths do I need to replace those lies with?

Today's Scripture Reference

"But prove yourselves doers of the word, and not merely hearers who delude themselves. For if anyone is a hearer of the word and not a doer, he is like a man who looks at his natural face in a mirror; for once he has looked at himself and gone away, he has immediately forgotten what kind of person he was. But one who looks intently at the perfect law, and law of liberty, and abides by it, not having become a forgetful hearer but an effectual doer, this man will be blessed in what he does."
—James 1:22–25 NASB

> "Immanuel . . . not only God with us, but God for us,
> God in us, God through us."
> —Dawn E. Stephenson, *Who Do You Say I Am?*

Immanuel

Draw What's on Your Heart

Day Three

The Practice of Abiding

Did you ever get grumbly about a thing? Turn it up full blast and get downright twisted in your knickers in it?

Newsflash . . . that's not freedom!

Ask Martha . . . you know, Mary's sister.

It was a BIG deal to have Jesus in town . . . let alone in your home.

Now this is where I could spin off in a thousand directions putting on a show myself. HGTV'ing in the name of ministry.

If I was showing up with radical candor, it may have been the reason I invited Immanuel in the first place. So I could make Martha Stewart envious. Make it all look glorious a thousand ways to Sunday.

So is it actually good, or does it simply look good in the picture on Ancient Insta.?

Here's the thing about freedom . . . the deep treasure Mary carried on the inside.

When Immanuel entered, God was with them. That was worthy of pause.

Watch this. See the one who spoke up all grumbly and knicker-twisted in Luke 10:40–42 TPT . . . spoiler alert. It wasn't Mary. She was sitting quietly practicing presence . . . in His presence, because this is where the peace was. Check it out as we enter into Martha's pity party:

"But Martha became exasperated by finishing the numerous household chores in preparation for her guests, so she interrupted Jesus and said, 'Lord, don't You think it's unfair that my sister left me to do all the work by myself? You should tell her to get up and help me.' The Lord answered her, 'Martha, my beloved Martha. Why are you upset and troubled, pulled away by all these many distractions? Are they really that important? Mary has discovered the one thing most important by choosing to sit at My feet. She is undistracted, and I won't take this privilege from her.'"

Mary was following the peace, Beloved. Mary sat at the feet of Shalom Himself. Mary basked in His rich deep voice. It filled her . . . from the inside out. So she could remain quiet in His love.

That right there . . . that's where the freedom is. Right at the feet of Jesus . . . abiding. Worshipping. This is for all the overproducers in the back rows. Read it again.

Because Mary, she knew a thing. Mary knew that if she filled up on worship, there would be plenty of all the other stuff that could be produced in a short amount of time, from her overflow of Him. No problem. The gold was in the worship.

Meanwhile Martha . . . Jesus lovingly untwists her and brings her back. Immanuel sings His freedom song over her – truth.

I don't know about you, Beloved, but the Martha in me just got a breakthrough. How many times have I made a thousand sandwiches that Jesus Himself never ordered?

That's not freedom . . . quite the contrary! That's bondage. Can you see it in Martha? More importantly, can you see it in you?

All the props and kudos that day went to Mary – the abider. The one who quietly sat at His feet. Hanging on Immanuel's every word . . . basking in His presence.

Mary knew, because she'd been sitting with Him often enough to know that when He was finished, Jesus could pull out enough loaves and fishes to feed the town and then some. And who's the wiser?

My prayer for you today, Beloved, is that you let Him fill you from the inside, overflowing to the outside, first.

Abide. Immanuel LOVES abiding. It is something that will never be taken from you.

Because when He's done filling the inside, Immanuel's got more than plenty to fill the outside too!

Prayers of Affirmation

Immanuel, Today I choose to bask in the richness of Your love. Today I choose to be still and know that You are God.

Scripture Reference: Psalm 46:10

Immanuel, Today, because You are with me, I am choosing to be overwhelmed by Your perfect love which will cast out any fear base that leads me to shift into performing; and robs me of the beauty of Your presence.
Scripture Reference: I John 4:18

Immanuel, I am grateful that in Your presence is fullness of joy, and at Your right hand are treasures forever more. Today, Immanuel, I choose the richness of Your presence.
Scripture Reference: Psalm 16:11

Come Up Higher Questions

1) How do I love You in truth today, Lord, in regard to this name?

2) Ask God if He can show you how to love yourself the way He loves you specifically in regard to this name.

3) In what tangible ways can I partner with this name of God to manifest Your presence more clearly in my daily life today, Lord?

4) What gift or talent (equipment or fruit of the Spirit) do I need to manifest this name of Yours on earth today, Lord?

5) Lord, is there anything more You would like to reveal to me about this name?

Today's Scripture Reference

"For the testimony of Jesus is the spirit of prophecy."
—Revelation 19:10b NASB

"But the fruit of the Spirit is love, joy, peace, patience, kindness, goodness, faithfulness, gentleness, self-control; against such things there is no law."
—Galatians 5:22–23 NASB

The Practice of Abiding

Draw What's on Your Heart

Day Four

The Battling Ear

"HE WHO HAS EARS TO HEAR, let him hear." Matthew 11:15 NASB

Simply put . . . there are just times we need to listen to the One who is always present! Note the quote from one of Ulysses S. Grant's Civil War Officers:

"This battle was fought with the ear, not the eye."

Forgive me, Lord, for the many times I've twirled ahead of You. Knowing You are always with me, I am anxiously basing decisions alone on what my eyes in front of me see.

Forgive me, Lord.

Our economy differs greatly from Immanuel's own – I wish I could begin to get the slightest grasp. What I've gleaned is that it is executed, often in a polar opposite framework, of our own economy here on earth. All of this, while Immanuel is at work through us; in this, our earthly kingdom. He splendidly operates in the duality of kingdoms and economies – His and ours.

We say, "Do! . . . and then do some more!" Immanuel says, "Sit at my feet and listen."

Remember Martha and Mary?

We say, "Success is being the top dog."

Immanuel says, "Truly, success is being a servant." Hmmmm . . . .

So when Immanuel says to sit and listen, perhaps we should pay attention. As the One who is always with us reroutes our neural pathways. Especially in the days in which we find ourselves.

If we are to win the thing, perhaps we need to be fighting some battles with our ears.

Jesus is quick to tell us in John 10:27 NLT, "My sheep hear my voice, I know them and they follow Me."

And when He has brought out all His sheep, He walks ahead of them and they will follow Him, for they are familiar with His voice. But they will run away from strangers and never follow them because they know it's a voice of a stranger." John 10:4–5 TPT

I'm sure we can agree, just as Mary was drawn to His voice first, that then led her to His feet. We need to learn to discern Immanuel's voice from among all the strange voices out there in this season.

It's the Shepherd Himself who guarantees our safety, as we follow and abide as He walks right beside us.

Today, Beloved, my prayer for you is that you can learn to discern His voice. That we each would stop long enough and make enough room in our lives to actually follow His voice. After all, it is Immanuel who leads us on the pathway of life.

Prayers of Affirmation

Immanuel, Today I am thankful that You are not just for Christmas, that You are here every second of every moment of every day. Thank you for Your promise that You will never leave us or forsake us. Today I invite You to invade my day with Your presence.
Scripture Reference: Hebrews 13:5

Immanuel, Today, because You are here, I don't have to lean on my own understanding of things. I can seek Your counsel, and You will make my ways straight.
Scripture Reference: Proverbs 3:5-6

Immanuel, There is nowhere that I can escape from Your presence. If I rose on the wings of the dawn, if I moved across the ocean Your hand would still be there to guide me; Your right hand to strengthen and support me.
Scripture Reference: Psalm 139:9-10

Come Up Higher Questions

1) How can I use this name of God to bring the kingdom of heaven to earth today, Lord?

2) How does this name of God contribute to the flourishing of my neighbors and city, Lord?

3) Lord, can You give me an encouraging word for another regarding this particular name through picture, scripture, song, or word?

4) Ask Him for any further clarification on the above word that He would like to share with you. Write it down. Share these words with that person.

5) Lord, what would You like to say to me today regarding this name that might encourage my own heart? Write it down.

Today's Scripture Reference

"Your kingdom come, Your will be done on earth as it is in heaven."
—Matthew 6:10 NASB

"Behold, I will do something new, now it will spring forth; will you not be aware of it? I will even make a roadway in the wilderness, rivers in the desert."
—Isaiah 43:19 NASB

IMMANUEL

The Battling Ear

Draw What's on Your Heart

Day Five

A Jonathan Friend

I'll never forget the day I got the unexpected call. Right as I was in the middle of the throes of my third move in four years . . . amidst all the other life changes and losses. About a week before departure. I'm not going to lie . . . this was HARD!

One of my favorite voices in the world was on the other end and said, "I'm making that trip with you. You're not doing that alone." Those ten words were worth 107.9 miles each (1,079 total miles) that I otherwise would have driven by myself (if you don't count the 100 lb. German Shepherd Gal and a cat).

My sweetest Christ Sister drove with her husband, four plus hours to get to me, spent the last weekend loading the moving trailer, cleaning the house, prepping and outfitting the car, doing dump runs, and all the other last minute things that had to be taken care of in a move. The next morning at 4 a.m., after bidding her husband farewell the night before, we set off on a three-day adventure . . . together.

Through the good, the funny, the ugly . . . on we trekked . . . together.

Immanuel. God with us. Just like my friend.

Immanuel's making the trip with us, wherever we're going . . . because Immanuel doesn't want us to be alone.

So God sent His Son, Jesus, to meet us, help us clean up our acts so we could move forward WITH Him.

So we don't have to travel alone. That's why Immanuel came for us.

Just like with my friend, I LOVE my adventures with Jesus. We are in "out of the way" places, sometimes we laugh, sometimes we cry, sometimes it's scary, but mostly because we're together we know it's ok. Not just because it's the two of us, but because Immanuel is right there with us.

Beloved, my prayer for you is that you know Immanuel . . . and cannot only know Him but pick up the phone and bring Immanuel to someone in need . . . in both big and little ways. Sometimes we are the only Immanuel people will ever see.

Is Immanuel with you today? Can you carry Immanuel to someone who needs Him today?

Are you ready? Speak these prayers over yourself when you are feeling alone.

Prayers of Affirmation

Immanuel, You are faithful, You are present, You are safe to trust.
Scripture Reference: Hebrews 13:5

Immanuel, You are strengthening me, You are helping me, You are upholding me with Your righteous right hand.
Scripture Reference: Isaiah 41:10

Immanuel, Thank you for coming from heaven for me, to dwell with us, to bring us to You eternally.
Scripture Reference: John 3:16

Come Up Higher Questions

1) Lord, what is the heart of this name of God towards me today?

2) Lord, is there anything else about the heart of this name of God towards me that I need to know or do today?

3) Lord, is there any area in my life in regard to this name in which I am out of obedience or susceptible to sin? Confess that area in the journal space provided.

4) Lord, what is the gift that You desire to give me in place of that area of weakness or disobedience that I can use to build Your kingdom?

5) Lord, what aspect of Your character or nature would You like to show me, in regard to this name, that I have not seen before?

Today's Scripture Reference

"Therefore there is now no condemnation for those who are in Christ Jesus."
—Romans 8:1 NASB

"What then shall we say to these things? If God is for us, who is against us? He who did not spare His own Son, but delivered Him over for us all, how will He not also with Him freely give us all things?"
—Romans 8:31-32 NASB

"If we confess our sins, He is faithful and righteous to forgive us our sins and to cleanse us from all unrighteousness."
—I John 1:9 NASB

IMMANUEL

A Jonathan Friend

Draw What's on Your Heart

Jehovah Jireh

The Lord Will Provide

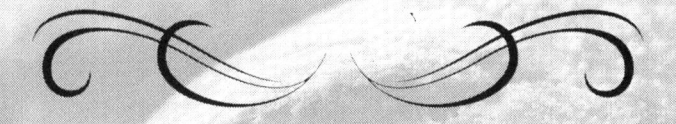

Victoriously I arise
Splendidly arrayed for battle
In the most magnificent spiritual armor
Straight from the hand of the God who Provides
Jehovah Jireh

Day One

Always A Step Ahead

I'm definitely no economist, but I know this. I LOVE to study God's economy.

Why, you may ask?

Mostly because I am constantly astounded by it when I see it in action.

Our needs are not a surprise to Him . . . not one of them. From the biggest to the smallest, every one of them has already been taken into account and supplied from eternity past. Those needs will appear answered right on time. He is never late! In Isaiah 65:24 NLT God says it this way:

"I will answer them before they even call to Me. While they are still talking about their needs, I will go ahead and answer their prayers!"

Get that . . . Jehovah Jireh doesn't leave us hopeless. That includes all the equipment and provision to carry out those plans ahead of time. Not to worry! He goes ahead of us!

Sometimes Jehovah Jireh waits till the eleventh hour, like in the case of Abraham and Isaac. As Abraham prepared to offer his son back to God, in obedience, as an offering on Mt. Moriah. (See Genesis 22). This is where we learn this name of God being used by a man of God with great faith.

From the time they left home and as they walked up that mountain, Abraham's mantra was "God will provide" as he thought about having to offer his son.

Did you ever have to talk to yourself that way? It is a conversation of BIG faith to take those steps in obedience.

Yet God's name IS His nature. If it is God Will Provide . . . then you can take that to the bank . . . or the mountain. And you can wait for your ram right there.

But here's the thing I've found about God's economy. The provision appears in the place He's called you to. It is activated by our obedience. Simply put . . .

Jehovah Jireh doesn't provide for or bless our disobedience.

So know this, Beloved! If you are walking in God's will, having done all that you know to do, come up against a need, you can praise that right in. Because that's what BIG faith does.

It is our "God-fidence" and His delight to show up when we are carrying out God's plans.

So that's my prayer for you today, Beloved, that you would come to learn and KNOW God as Jehovah Jireh as you walk out the path He has for you.

So I'm not sure if it's a ram you need today, but Jehovah Jireh's storehouses are full. He is waiting to swing open the doors for you. Position yourselves to receive.

Are you ready? If not, pray these prayers over yourself until you are.

Prayers of Affirmation

Jehovah Jireh, Today I am choosing to submit and humble myself under Your mighty hand. I submit to Your plans and purposes for my life today. In that place, I am secure in knowing that You will provide all of my needs according to Your riches in glory.
Scripture Reference: I Peter 5:6, Philippians 4:19

Jehovah Jireh, Thank you that I have EVERY. SINGLE. RESOURCE. I need to carry out Your will, plans, and purposes for my life today. You did not spare Your own Son on my account. There is nothing missing or lacking because of Your great love for me.
Scripture Reference: Romans 8:32

Jehovah Jireh, I am a cattle baron's daughter. You who own the cattle on a thousand hills will make sure that I possess all that I need. I thank you that You came that we may have abundant life in You.
Scripture Reference: Psalm 50:10, John 10:10

Come Up Higher Questions

1) Based on Hebrews 10:35–39, Where have I cast away my confidence in Your name here, Lord?

2) Where am I specifically drawing back in my knowledge of this name, Lord, purposefully not looking at things I need to see? Open my eyes to any blind spots I have to You regarding this name. Confess what He shows you.

3) Where specifically am I in need of endurance regarding this name, Lord?

4) What lies have I been believing about You pertaining to this name, Lord?
   What lies have I been believing about myself pertaining to this name, Lord?
   Confess those lies by writing them down in the journal pages and offer them back to Him.

5) Ask Him what truths He would like to replace those lies with regarding this name. Write those down in the journal pages that follow.

Today's Scripture Reference

"Therefore, do not throw away Your confidence, which has a great reward. For you have need of endurance, so that when you have done the will of God, you may receive what was promised. For yet in a very little while, He who is coming will come, and will not delay. But my righteous one shall live by faith; and if he shrinks back, my soul has no pleasure in him. But we are not of those who shrink back to destruction, but of those who have faith to the preserving of the soul."

—Hebrews 10:35–39 NASB

Jehovah Jireh

Draw What's on Your Heart

Day Two

Covenants and Contracts

NEGOTIATIONS, WINS, LOSSES, VICTORIES, LESSONS. Gifts in the agreements that are penned. The places we won, the places we get educated for next time.

Contracts and Covenants – the constructs of life. In business, it's an everyday part of every day! It's how we get things done.

In God's upside-down economy, things look a bit different. Let's take a look.

I always say, I know when God is negotiating in the details of a contract – there isn't a winner and loser. There are two winners – a win/win is the telltale sign He's been involved.

Jehovah Jireh – The Ultimate Winner of it all. It's all His. Jehovah Jireh could take His proverbial toys and head home anytime He wants . . . but Jehovah Jireh has a covenant with us. Jehovah Jireh's been providing for us since Genesis 1:1 and will through Revelation 22:21. We can take that to the bank, Beloved!

Watch the Art of the Deal – it pays to pay attention to how God does the thing, because we've all been on the losing side once or twice, am I right?

Way back in the Garden, Adam and Eve made a bad trade. They handed their authority over to the enemy . . . so in that moment, Satan got exactly what he went after . . . power AND authority to rule this broken world. That authority that had previously belonged to Adam and Eve was handed over in one bad, quick instant. (See Genesis 1 for all the deets on that).

Way back then, God knew that would never do – not to His Beloveds. So God foretells of the day when all will be set right . . . by Jehovah Jireh. His answer to that was Jesus, prototyped to Abraham and Isaac in Genesis 22, as the "Sacrificial Lamb." Go read about that.

In a glorious power play – Jesus dies, resurrects, and with His DUNAMIS Power (resurrection power), Jesus hands us back our authority over the enemy.

Jesus seats us with Him in the heavenlies.

Jehovah Jireh – The Lord DID Provide . . . Jehovah Jireh is still providing for us today, each and every day, in the little and the huge.

Beloved, I am praying that you make your own glorious power swap with Jehovah Jireh today. That you push fear, stress, anxiety, anger, resentment, all the ugly committed against you . . . (go ahead and fill in your own blank) back, push it across the table to the One who paid dearly to have it. Take back the authority Jehovah Jireh is offering you in this glorious power swap. The authority over the enemy to lead a victorious life over all the messes . . . each and every one. That is ONE GLORIOUS WIN / WIN! Jehovah Jireh . . .

Now, go take your seat! Are you ready? If not, pray these prayers over yourself until you are.

Prayers of Affirmation

Jehovah Jireh, I am not partnering with fear any longer. I take authority over that and move forward with Jehovah Jireh in the power, love, and sound, sound mind that Christ died for me to walk in.

Scripture Reference: II Timothy 1:7

Jehovah Jireh, I have been chosen by Him to be redeemed. In exchange for anger, bitterness, malice, unforgiveness, I power swap for the tenderhearted mercy, kindness, humility, gentleness, patience that He died for me to receive.

Scripture Reference: Colossians 3:12

Jehovah Jireh, There is not a need of mine that You don't know about, that You haven't already accounted and provided for. Before I even asked, it was done.

Scripture Reference: Isaiah 65:24

Come Up Higher Questions

1) Lord, would You give me an opportunity to apply the knowledge of this name in my life today?

2) Lord, can You show me what You see in my applying this name today?

3) Lord, can You show me the treasure that You have placed in this person / situation in which I will be applying this name today?

4) What lies have I believed here that I need to break agreement with today in regard to this name / person / situation?

5) What truths do I need to replace those lies with?

Today's Scripture Reference

"But prove yourselves doers of the word, and not merely hearers who delude themselves. For if anyone is a hearer of the word and not a doer, he is like a man who looks at his natural face in a mirror; for once he has looked at himself and gone away, he has immediately forgotten what kind of person he was. But one who looks intently at the perfect law, and law of liberty, and abides by it, not having become a forgetful hearer but an effectual doer, this man will be blessed in what he does."
—James 1:22–25 NASB

Jehovah Jireh

COVENANTS AND CONTRACTS

Draw What's on Your Heart

Day Three

Faithful

I've always been smitten by sunrises. Double bonus if they are occurring over water. Perhaps it's the "diamonds" spinning and dancing from the sun's rays. I've always interpreted that fiery sparkle as a chorus of praise awakening with that rising ball of fire.

So when God told me, "I want you to go watch the sunrise." I was happy to oblige. It was a gift to sit out on my patio daily overlooking the lake with a bird's eye view of my heavenly Father's handiwork. What I didn't know was that I was about to be schooled in so much more about its Maker. Thus began the journey last Spring that has spawned a thousand lessons and deepened my faith at new levels.

Every morning I dutifully asked Alexa, "What time is sunrise?" Every morning it seemed to creep a minute earlier until summer solstice. When it started to adjust to a minute later. Fascinating.

Jehovah Jireh . . . showing me that He has an intricate order to things embedded in His sun . . . and the Son. Both are by design . . . Just like clockwork.

Jehovah Jireh's timing is impeccable. He is not a nano-second late. The earth's continuation to spin on its axis is dependent on this very fact.

Some mornings as I worked out, waiting in the silence, grounding myself in the present moment, the sky would be a spectacular show of changing cloud colors the likes of which Crayola could not imagine. Other mornings there was a monotone to the sky that allowed Jehovah Jireh to rise and very simply, quietly, lovingly provide the light that rises up and overcomes my darkness.

Either way, Jehovah Jireh. He proves consistently faithful to bring His overcoming light with Him . . . for us . . . for our healing . . . for Jehovah Jireh's glory.

Every day I show up, it's a surprise to see exactly where along the shoreline the shifting beams of light will enter the horizon but one thing is sure: They will show up! Just like His own Son, Jehovah Jireh consistently arrives at the appointed hour. He does for all of His Beloveds, since the beginning of time . . . all the way to the end. You can take that to the bank.

Are you ready to believe that truth about Jehovah Jireh today? If not, speak the prayers below over yourself until you are.

Prayers of Affirmation

Jehovah Jireh, All the animals of the forest are Yours . . . all the birds on the mountains and the animals of the fields as well. In thankfulness and faithfulness I come to You . . . in the middle of "a thing", I call to You. Your promise, Jehovah Jireh, is to rescue me. My promise to You is that I will give You all the glory. Together, Jehovah Jireh, is how we win the thing.
Scripture Reference: Psalm 50:10-15

Jehovah Jireh, Before we call, You answer. While we are yet speaking (the thing), You hear.
Scripture Reference: Isaiah 65:24

Jehovah Jireh, You are faithful and I can trust You to supply all my needs. However, the most valuable of Your provision in my life, aside from Your Son, is Your peace.
Scripture Reference: Philippians 4:6-7

Come Up Higher Questions

1) How do I love You in truth today, Lord, in regard to this name?

2) Ask God if He can show you how to love yourself the way He loves you specifically in regard to this name.

3) In what tangible ways can I partner with this name of God to manifest Your presence more clearly in my daily life today, Lord?

4) What gift or talent (equipment or fruit of the Spirit) do I need to manifest this name of Yours on earth today, Lord?

5) Lord, is there anything more You would like to reveal to me about this name?

Today's Scripture Reference

"For the testimony of Jesus is the spirit of prophecy."
—Revelation 19:10b NASB

"But the fruit of the Spirit is love, joy, peace, patience, kindness, goodness, faithfulness, gentleness, self-control; against such things there is no law."
—Galatians 5:22-23 NASB

Jehovah Jireh

Draw What's on Your Heart

Day Four

The Heart of the Giver

To the couple that bought a truck for the purpose of helping people move.

To the family that bought that vacation house to provide a respite for many – with a special eye toward those families that could never afford, nor had ever been on, a vacation.

To the people who drive ten hours round trip to assist the broken, single lady with her moving sale.

THANK YOU!! It seems trite and too insignificant simply to format eight letters, two words, to express the value of your service. Enter the bigger picture.

Enter Jehovah Jireh – The Lord Will Provide.

Let's really let this sink in. That provision . . . all that "providing", of all of those needs that are screaming all around us . . . Jehovah Jireh's heart is to partner with us to share the wealth He so graciously entrusted within us. Jehovah Jireh calls us to BE the blessing to His people . . . and we're all His people. Jehovah Jireh calls us to remember nothing that we actually "own" is ours. It's on loan to us to figure out how to use it to build His kingdom. Jehovah Jireh takes that "joyful giver" thing very seriously.

Nothing meant more to me in my own darkest hours than the one who simply wrote me a check – no strings attached.

Driving down the driveway into the unknown, to escape, with everything uncertain except the $200 in my pocket . . . yes, that was brave. Having to be the helper turned recipient, that was certainly the most humbling and definitely the bravest of all. Learning to receive the kindness of Jehovah Jireh through the hands of His people is a lesson I will never forget.

See how that works?

Beloved, it is my prayer for you today that you do. That on whichever side of the equation you may find yourself in this hour – be it the Giver or the Receiver – that you would walk that position out honorably for the sake of Jehovah Jireh – the Lord Will Provide. Give freely, as the hands and feet of Jehovah Jireh, to bless another. Receive with gratitude from the heart of Jehovah Jireh Himself. That you recognize the humility of both positions. In the giving, that Jehovah Jireh would choose to entrust us with His resources. More astounding, that Jehovah Jireh would choose to partner with us in anything, much less bringing His kingdom to earth. In the receiving, Jehovah Jireh would seek us out to bless us through the hands of another.

Can you see it? Can you receive it? If not, repeat these prayers over yourself until you can.

Prayers of Affirmation

Jehovah Jireh, You are Our Provider. You have never, nor will You ever, lack for any resource. It's all Yours. You move those resources through my very own hands and feet. Thank you for wanting to partner with me.
Scripture Reference: Psalm 50, Psalm 34:10

Jehovah Jireh, Even now Your eyes are searching for those whose hearts are dedicated to You, to strengthen them. Strengthen me, Lord, so that I can be an honorable partner of Yours in both giving and receiving.
Scripture Reference: II Chronicles 16:9

Jehovah Jireh, Thank you that You enable me to be a cheerful giver. I don't have to give out of compulsion or reluctance that there is lack or shortage in Your Kingdom. I can give freely, because I have received freely. There is NO shortage in Your Kingdom.
Scripture Reference: II Corinthians 9:6–8, Matthew 10:8

Come Up Higher Questions

1) How can I use this name of God to bring the kingdom of heaven to earth today, Lord?

2) How does this name of God contribute to the flourishing of my neighbors and city, Lord?

3) Lord, can You give me an encouraging word for another regarding this particular name through picture, scripture, song, or word?

4) Ask Him for any further clarification on the above word that He would like to share with you. Write it down. Share these words with that person.

5) Lord, what would You like to say to me today regarding this name that might encourage my own heart? Write it down.

Today's Scripture Reference

"Your kingdom come, Your will be done on earth as it is in heaven."
—Matthew 6:10 NASB

"Behold, I will do something new, now it will spring forth; will you not be aware of it? I will even make a roadway in the wilderness, rivers in the desert."
—Isaiah 43:19 NASB

Jehovah Jireh

The Heart of the Giver

Draw What's on Your Heart

Day Five

Unto The Lamb

FLIPPING THE PAGES OF SCRIPTURE one cannot help but be drawn to all of the provision that happens from Genesis 1:1 through Revelation 22:21, it's all a thread of His gracious provision towards us, His people.

In every situation in which biblical characters found themselves immersed, Jehovah Jireh came through to provide a way through. It is the same in our lives today. In every situation in which we can find ourselves immersed, Jehovah Jireh has already made provision for the way through.

However, no provision is more significant than the Son of God Himself shedding His blood for the redemption of our sin. Jehovah Jireh orchestrating our way back from hell. Not just a one-time buy back in the afterlife, NO! I'm talking about the blood of the Lamb that redeems us from death daily . . . here on earth in this life.

Jehovah Jireh, offering us moment-by-moment, the Lamb of God who takes away the sin of the world. It is His offering, this perfect Lamb, that allows us to escape the hell of our own making daily, here on earth. This same blood allows us to boldly approach the Throne of Grace as righteous heirs, seated next to Him in the high, heavenly places. It is from here that we can walk God-fidently, victoriously through life daily. The same provision that allows us to bring God's will to be done on earth as it is in heaven.

Beloved, is this not mind-baffling to you? We carry Him and heaven with us as its ambassadors because of Jehovah Jireh's provision. This earth is the only glimpse of hell His children will ever catch. For those who don't take advantage of His provision, this earth is the only glimpse of heaven they'll ever be privileged enough to glimpse.

I don't know about you, but that's cause for worship. Let's thank that precious Lamb of God today. Let's give glory to Jehovah Jireh.

Most importantly, do you believe? Are you ready? If not, pray these prayers over yourself today.

Prayers of Affirmation

Jehovah Jireh, Today I want the best gift of all that You have provided in Your Son, Jesus Christ. Lord, not only the provision of eternal life, but abundant life in the here and now.

Today, Father, I will behold the Lamb of God who takes away the sins of the world.
Scripture Reference: John 3:16, John 1:29

Jehovah Jireh, You who knew no sin became sin so we could become the righteousness of God. I thank you for Your righteousness. It is the foundational provision that allows me to come to You.
Scripture Reference: II Corinthians 5:21

Jehovah Jireh, Thank you that the provision of the blood of the Lamb allows us to be seated with You in the heavenlies. Thank you that we are joint heirs of Christ. Thank you for all of the power and authority of Christ that we walk in because of this provision.
Scripture Reference: Ephesians 2:6, Romans 8:17, Luke 10:19

Come Up Higher Questions

1) Lord, what is the heart of this name of God towards me today?

2) Lord, is there anything else about the heart of this name of God towards me that I need to know or do today?

3) Lord, is there any area in my life in regard to this name in which I am out of obedience or susceptible to sin? Confess that area in the journal space provided.

4) Lord, what is the gift that You desire to give me in place of that area of weakness or disobedience that I can use to build Your kingdom?

5) Lord, what aspect of Your character or nature would You like to show me, in regard to this name, that I have not seen before?

Today's Scripture Reference

"Therefore there is now no condemnation for those who are in Christ Jesus."

—Romans 8:1 NASB

"What then shall we say to these things? If God is for us, who is against us? He who did not spare His own Son, but delivered Him over for us all, how will He not also with Him freely give us all things?"

—Romans 8:31–32 NASB

"If we confess our sins, He is faithful and righteous to forgive us our sins and to cleanse us from all unrighteousness."

—I John 1:9 NASB

Jehovah Jireh

Unto The Lamb

Draw What's on Your Heart

Jehovah Shalom

The Lord Is Peace

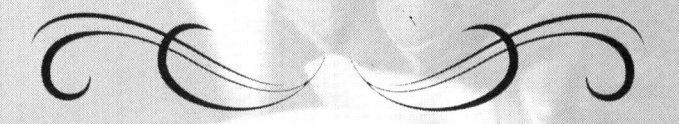

Victoriously I arise
To enter the sacred space of His peace
A mighty fortress
The place where all is whole, complete,
Nothing missing, nothing broken
The presence of Jehovah Shalom

Day One

Let's Roll

When God says it's time to do a thing . . . let's roll.

When Jesus told the disciples to get into a boat, they would be heading to the other side . . . Jesus was so secure in that directive to them that He curled up in a ball and decided it was time to nap.

Then the storm . . . I'm sure the disciples were thinking, "Wait!! He didn't say anything about a storm!"

Sleeping . . . versus panicking. Because you know . . . the storm.

Those storms, our trials or traumas, they shift our gaze, they hold us captive to their winds – sometimes they are outside and sometimes they are the storms of our own thinking.

The noise of the waves pounding against the boat . . . or in our head. They are heaving and hurling us all over, knocking us down . . . it makes us forget His words . . .

"We're going to the other side."

Because in Jehovah Shalom's world, there is no storm strong enough to disrupt the plan.

Perhaps some great learning opportunities, but still scheduled to arrive right on time.

And that's why the disciples know to run to Him . . . because they have lots yet to learn.

They could have stilled that same storm . . . but they forgot for a hot second who they were, whose they were, because . . . the waves and the wind.

When Jesus spoke into the storm, it had no choice but to obey . . . "Peace! Be still!" Both wind and waves know their Maker.

So my prayer over the wind and waves of your life today, is "Peace! Be still!!"

Speak those words to the waves that come crashing in around you . . . so many in 2020.

Tell the wind to back off! It's the wind that makes the waves.

Will you do that today? Are you ready? If not, say these prayers over yourself until you are.

Prayers of Affirmation

Jehovah Shalom, Today I choose not to get caught up in the "group think" of the people around me, like the disciples on the boat. Today, I choose to use all of the power and authority that You died to give me to still my storm.
Scripture Reference: Luke 10:19

Jehovah Shalom, Today I choose to use my "mustard seed" faith to plant a new beginning. I choose to break the cycle of fear, anxiety, and unbelief. Today, I choose Your Shalom.
Scripture Reference: Matthew 17:20

Jehovah Shalom, Today I choose to believe that You are who You say You are. You are Jehovah Shalom. I receive Your peace.
Scripture Reference: Mark 6:29

Come Up Higher Questions

1) Based on Hebrews 10:35–39, Where have I cast away my confidence in Your name here, Lord?

2) Where am I specifically drawing back in my knowledge of this name, Lord, purposefully not looking at things I need to see? Open my eyes to any blind spots I have to You regarding this name. Confess what He shows you.

3) Where specifically am I in need of endurance regarding this name, Lord?

4) What lies have I been believing about You pertaining to this name, Lord?
   What lies have I been believing about myself pertaining to this name, Lord?
   Confess those lies by writing them down in the journal pages and offer them back to Him.

5) Ask Him what truths He would like to replace those lies with regarding this name. Write those down in the journal pages that follow.

Today's Scripture Reference

"Therefore, do not throw away Your confidence, which has a great reward. For you have need of endurance, so that when you have done the will of God, you may receive what was promised. For yet in a very little while, He who is coming will come, and will not delay. But my righteous one shall live by faith; and if he shrinks back, my soul has no pleasure in him. But we are not of those who shrink back to destruction, but of those who have faith to the preserving of the soul."

—Hebrews 10:35–39 NASB

Jehovah Shalom

Let's Roll

Draw What's on Your Heart

Day Two

The Wheat and the Chaff

IF YOU'VE BEEN ON PLANET EARTH the past few months, it's easy to recognize that one thing we are missing more than health, jobs, security, joy, and status quo is this – PEACE.

Many feel like they are being crushed, pressed, shaken to their core, stripped, and even attacked.

Whew . . . that's quite a laundry list.

If it were a media production, I think it would be titled "A World Run Amuck."

But see, Beloved, that's where we have an ally, an advocate, a Kinsman Redeemer.

And today He promises to show up for us as Jehovah Shalom – God IS our peace.

Remember . . . His name IS His nature. It's not something He has . . . it's WHO HE IS!! Sit with that for a second.

Can you use some Shalom today? In Hebrew, the translation is whole, complete, nothing missing, nothing broken.

The first time we see this name it is used by Gideon in Judges 6:12–14. Suffice to say, Gideon's world looked a lot like ours. Only their virus was an enemy, people who had tortured the Israelites relentlessly. They held them hostage, they stole their resources. The Israelites were literally surrounded by the Midianites. Some of us realize the magnitude of this type of enemy.

Yet when God Himself shows up to reveal His plan of victory for Israel, He has to go into a wine press to find Gideon . . . because Gideon's hiding in there . . . quaking and shaking . . . trying to protect and thresh what little wheat (food) he had.

Well, Beloved, here's a thing you need to know about wheat. You don't thresh it in a wine press, unless you're terrified of your enemy. It's beaten outside . . . in the open air, so the wind can blow away the chaff and leave the grain.

But see . . . here's the thing about God.

He loves the visual.

When Jehovah Shalom came to Gideon that day, it was to blow away the cowardly chaff of Gideon's life. God was after the grain of Gideon's heart.

God had to come down to make an appearance . . . to call Gideon into the purpose He created Gideon to walk in.

But first, He needed to give him His peace. How can we be who we are called to be while we are all bound up and reside in fear?

So God says, "The Lord is with you, O Valiant Warrior!" . . . wait . . . what?

What did God just say?

Did God call Gideon a Valiant Warrior?

The guy on the floor of the winepress threshing wheat?

Yes! You see, the grain of Gideon . . . Gideon's purpose that he was created to fulfill, was that of a Valiant Warrior. God saw it in Gideon. God sees it in you. So God uses His words to call it out of Gideon.

But first, Beloved, Jehovah Shalom has to deliver His peace to you before Jehovah Shalom can send you out to fulfill your purpose in this crazy world.

So I'd encourage you to read about Gideon in Judges 6. Watch the victories he accumulates once Gideon finds his peace and centers in it. It was Gideon who called God "Jehovah Shalom" first.

Today, Beloved, my prayer for you is that you let Jehovah Shalom find you in your wine press. I encourage you to let Him deliver to you His peace – the place where there is nothing missing, nothing broken, you are whole, complete . . .

Yes! Even in the middle of the crazy world in which we find ourselves today.

My prayer is you listen as Jehovah Shalom calls your name.

Are you ready? If not, pray these prayers over yourself until you are.

Prayers of Affirmation

Jehovah Shalom, I confess that in the past I have found myself misplacing my worship at the altar of fear. Forgive me. Today, I am a new creature in Christ. The old has passed away, and all things are new. Today, I choose Your peace.
Scripture Reference: II Corinthians 5:17

Jehovah Shalom, Your peace light shines into my fear darkness, and my fear darkness cannot overcome it. Today, I will radiate Your peace light.
Scripture Reference: John 1:5

Jehovah Shalom, Your peace brings me the strength I need to overcome. You are my light and my salvation. Whom shall I fear? You are the strength of my life; of whom shall I be afraid?
Scripture Reference: Psalm 27:1

Come Up Higher Questions

1) Lord, would You give me an opportunity to apply the knowledge of this name in my life today?

2) Lord, can You show me what You see in my applying this name today?

3) Lord, can You show me the treasure that You have placed in this person / situation in which I will be applying this name today?

4) What lies have I believed here that I need to break agreement with today in regard to this name / person / situation?

5) What truths do I need to replace those lies with?

Today's Scripture Reference

"But prove yourselves doers of the word, and not merely hearers who delude themselves. For if anyone is a hearer of the word and not a doer, he is like a man who looks at his natural face in a mirror; for once he has looked at himself and gone away, he has immediately forgotten what kind of person he was. But one who looks intently at the perfect law, and law of liberty, and abides by it, not having become a forgetful hearer but an effectual doer, this man will be blessed in what he does."

—James 1:22–25 NASB

Draw What's on Your Heart

Day Three

The Good Shepherd

There are days I relate fully to the sheep analogy Jesus uses for us continually throughout scripture. They are a simple creature. I know this . . . I'm always grateful that He's the faithful Shepherd ever on guard to maintain peace amongst the flock.

Sheep were designed by God to be 100 percent dependent on their Good Shepherd . . . so were we. Like the sheep, we were created to dwell in His pasture of peace. A place, like His name, where all is whole, complete, nothing missing, nothing broken. I've pondered oftentimes, if that wasn't the main purpose He created sheep, so we would have a visual. Perhaps we could be offended at the sheep analogy . . . but wait. Consider Jesus trying to explain the concept of Himself as the Ruling Messiah, Suffering Servant to the disciples THREE times in the gospel of Mark . . . which ends up netting Jesus telling Peter, "Get behind me, Satan!" (Mark 8:33). Truly the concepts of the Divine are far beyond our reach. Sheep. Yes, makes sense.

Have you ever been given an assignment, a dream, a vision for something He's creating for you to do? You've gotten so excited, danced around about how fun it is, and then said . . . "I CAN'T DO THAT!!! THAT'S WAY TOO BIG!!"

Voice of the sheep . . . sounds like bleating to the ear of the Shepherd. Something coming against His flock. Perhaps it's one of their biggest enemies, fear!

Enter Jehovah Shalom. To run towards His sheep . . . you . . . me.

Gently Jehovah Shalom picks us up and says, "I am here. Nothing harms my flock here in My pasture of peace! This thing I am asking of you, do not let fear rob you of the joy of the assignment. In My pasture of peace, all is made possible because I will do it through you. I am leading. Follow Me. Step by step we will go together. Look only at one important step . . . the next step. Don't run ahead of Me (as sheep are prone to do).

No, keep cadence with Me. Don't lag or linger in the distant past, or bound ahead into the fearful future, no . . . remain with Me in the eternal present."

Beloved, it is here we are safest. In His arms of grace, tucked into the eternal present, standing steadfast in the pasture of peace with Jehovah Shalom Himself. Let Him whisper to you each step of the way as Jehovah Shalom leads you beside still waters. As Jehovah Shalom restores your soul.

Walk honorably beside the Good Shepherd diligently obedient to His voice wrapped in the peace of Jehovah Shalom. He leads us in pathways of life (no death there), into Jehovah Shalom's presence where there is fullness of joy and at His right hand treasures forever. Yes . . . step by loving step. Until with Jehovah Shalom, we win that gigantic thing!!

So my prayer for you today, Beloved, is that you pick up Jehovah Shalom's hand as He extends it to you. That you recognize that with and through His shalom all things are possible. That you walk honorably with Jehovah Shalom today in the eternal present . . . one step at a time.

Are you ready to believe and receive that His shalom is yours today? If not, pray these prayers until you can.

Prayers of Affirmation

Jehovah Shalom, Today I believe that with You beside me, working through me with Your shalom, I can do all things through Christ who strengthens me.
Scripture Reference: Philippians 4:13

Jehovah Shalom, Today I receive the peace that You died for me to walk in. Together we will walk in Your shalom, which is unlike anything the world has to offer.
Scripture Reference: John 14:27

Jehovah Shalom, Today I confess the times when I have partnered with the inferior covenant of fear. I am thankful that when we confess our sins, You quickly forgive us and restore us to Your Shalom.
Scripture Reference: I John 1:9

Come Up Higher Questions

1) How do I love You in truth today, Lord, in regard to this name?

2) Ask God if He can show you how to love yourself the way He loves you specifically in regard to this name.

3) In what tangible ways can I partner with this name of God to manifest Your presence more clearly in my daily life today, Lord?

4) What gift or talent (equipment or fruit of the Spirit) do I need to manifest this name of Yours on earth today, Lord?

5) Lord, is there anything more You would like to reveal to me about this name?

Today's Scripture Reference

"For the testimony of Jesus is the spirit of prophecy."
—Revelation 19:10b NASB

"But the fruit of the Spirit is love, joy, peace, patience, kindness, goodness, faithfulness, gentleness, self-control; against such things there is no law."
—Galatians 5:22–23 NASB

Jehovah Shalom

The Good Shepherd

Draw What's on Your Heart

Day Four

Upsetting the Peace Cart

Ever have a day where a thing is gnawing at your heart – I mean clawing away to get in and flip your "peace cart" . . . like total the whole dang thing!

Enter Jehovah Shalom – The Lord IS Peace (emphasis mine).

Watch how this works: Because God IS peace, Jehovah Shalom doesn't simply say, "Peace I leave with you; My Peace I give to you; not as the world gives, do I give to you."

Let not your heart be troubled, nor let it be fearful . . . these things I have spoken to you, that IN ME (emphasis mine) you may have peace. In the world you will have tribulation, but take courage; I have overcome the world." John 14:27, 16:33

Jehovah Shalom IS that peace. So what Jehovah Shalom's saying is He is giving us Himself (when we are doing our part of abiding IN ME – Jesus) we experience the benefit of more of Him. More Jehovah Shalom. So we are able to maintain the calm in the storm, the unwavering faith. Press deeper into Him.

Jehovah Shalom is pretty clear on the "in this world we will have trouble" part. But press in, Beloved, Jehovah Shalom has overcome the world. My prayer for you is that you reflect His Shalom to a broken, chaotic world. Jehovah Shalom is inviting you to carry Him with you today – what an honor and a privilege to bring His Shalom wherever you go today.

Are you ready? If not, say these prayers over yourself today. This is you. This is Jehovah Shalom.

Prayers of Affirmation

Jehovah Shalom, I walk in peace and cast out fear because You have not given me a spirit of fear, but of power, and of love, and a sound, sound mind.
Scripture Reference: II Timothy 1:7

Jehovah Shalom, I am taking Your courage today, and walking in it along with Your peace. Because You dwell in and with me, Lord. Today, in all things, we will move in accordance to Your will. You have already overcome all things. Today we walk in the victory You have secured for us. I receive that victory today.
Scripture Reference: John 16:33

Jehovah Shalom, Your name is a strong tower. I run into it, and I am safe.
Scripture Reference: Proverbs 18:10

Come Up Higher Questions

1) How can I use this name of God to bring the kingdom of heaven to earth today, Lord?

2) How does this name of God contribute to the flourishing of my neighbors and city, Lord?

3) Lord, can You give me an encouraging word for another regarding this particular name through picture, scripture, song, or word?

4) Ask Him for any further clarification on the above word that He would like to share with you. Write it down. Share these words with that person.

5) Lord, what would You like to say to me today regarding this name that might encourage my own heart? Write it down.

Today's Scripture Reference

"Your kingdom come, Your will be done on earth as it is in heaven."
—Matthew 6:10 NASB

"Behold, I will do something new, now it will spring forth; will you not be aware of it? I will even make a roadway in the wilderness, rivers in the desert."
—Isaiah 43:19 NASB

> "But press in, Beloved, Jehovah Shalom has overcome the world."
> —Dawn E. Stephenson, *Who Do You Say I Am?*

Jehovah Shalom

Draw What's on Your Heart

Day Five

The Weaponry of Jehovah Shalom

In our culture of the "productive", we might find the concept of "peaceful rest" as a weapon of warfare, well . . . odd.

Or is it?

Enter Jehovah Shalom.

See back in Exodus 31:13 God and Moses were chatting up on Mt. Sinai. God spoke to Moses of the Sabbath and that he was to teach the Israelites how important it was to set apart a day of peaceful rest because it honored Him. The Sabbath was so close to His own heart and important that God Himself built it into the model of creation. God's grand finale creation, Adam, was created on day six and from there, after pronouncing Adam good, God and Adam entered a peaceful Sabbath rest to experience Jehovah Shalom.

Did you catch that? Adam was born and went right into the Shalom of Sabbath the next day! It was a rhythm God would establish in order to draw His people to Himself, because God loves and favors us and desires our company . . . the Shalom of the Sabbath. Understand, like hosting the presence of Jehovah Shalom Himself, the shalom of Sabbath is like hitting a reset button in our lives. It restores the very essence of Jehovah Shalom Himself.

Jehovah Shalom wants to remind us that in this world there is nothing that can offer a peace like His. So in God's grace, God created a sacred day of restoration in which we are to draw up under the wing of Jehovah Shalom to find our shalom. A place where the cares of this world can't breathe.

Jehovah Shalom wants to remind us that putting aside the hustle and bustle, stepping away from the crazy intentionally requires a discipline that has become foreign as a culture to us. It is not foreign to Jehovah Shalom. It is that very discipline that is seen as an act of worship, a concerted effort that says to God, "I trust that it is You who is able to deliver a peace to me that the world cannot understand. Your name is Your nature, and I hunger to spend time in Your presence."

The enemy takes no greater joy than getting us in a twist by cramming every second of our schedules, robbing us of our shalom. The enemy gets us to grab the bait that says, "That's not enough, you've got to DO more, be busier, earn more, BE more." Quite the antithesis of the rest provided through Jehovah Shalom, right?

Important to know that the concept of rest we are provided through Jehovah Shalom, then, may be considered one of our best weapons of warfare in our spiritual arsenal. To spend time in the company of Jehovah Shalom is what enables us to stand firm in His peace, to carry God's peace with us wherever we go, and to leave that same peace behind when we depart.

Today my prayer for you, Beloved, is that your peace sandals are double knotted. That they won't fall off. That no one steals them from you. Go forth, then, in His shalom.

Are you ready? If not, pray these prayers over yourself until you are.

Prayers of Affirmation

Jehovah Shalom, You lead me in pathways of peace, beside still waters. With Your shalom You restore my soul. Today I receive the rest that accompanies Your presence.
Scripture Reference: Psalm 23

Jehovah Shalom, In You I find a fortress in which I will never be shaken. You provide a place in which I can wait safely and quietly before You, in hope. I thank you today, Lord, that You are my refuge where no enemy can reach me.
Scripture Reference: Psalm 62

Lord, My soul can return to its shalom, its rest, because You have dealt bountifully with me. You reward me fully with Your shalom because I have put my trust in You.
Scripture Reference: Psalm 116

Come Up Higher Questions

1) Lord, what is the heart of this name of God towards me today?

2) Lord, is there anything else about the heart of this name of God towards me that I need to know or do today?

3) Lord, is there any area in my life in regard to this name in which I am out of obedience or susceptible to sin? Confess that area in the journal space provided.

4) Lord, what is the gift that You desire to give me in place of that area of weakness or disobedience that I can use to build Your kingdom?

5) Lord, what aspect of Your character or nature would You like to show me, in regard to this name, that I have not seen before?

Today's Scripture Reference

"Therefore there is now no condemnation for those who are in Christ Jesus."
—Romans 8:1 NASB

"What then shall we say to these things? If God is for us, who is against us? He who did not spare His own Son, but delivered Him over for us all, how will He not also with Him freely give us all things?"
—Romans 8:31–32 NASB

"If we confess our sins, He is faithful and righteous to forgive us our sins and to cleanse us from all unrighteousness."
—I John 1:9 NASB

Jehovah Shalom

The Weaponry of Jehovah Shalom

Draw What's on Your Heart

Jehovah Shammah

The Lord Is There

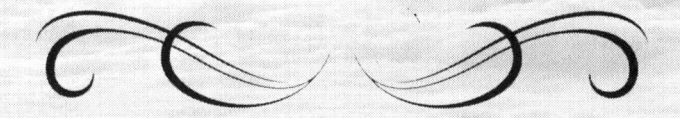

Victoriously I arise
To take Your hand,
To wield the weaponry of Your presence
In every battle for my wholeness
O Jehovah Shammah
You are here
I am who You say I am
Today I believe

I am whole

Amen

Day One

Not Alone

HAVE YOU EVER BEEN LONELY? Felt unseen? Unheard? Been abandoned? Unknown?

In real life, these things are experienced by many daily. In Daily Life 2020, with so much at stake and in flux in our own spinning orbits, it is easy to let people slip between the cracks.

Many are experiencing grief at different altitudes. As a society we are seeing collective grief – meaning we are all in the same "grief pool" processing differently – at unprecedented levels.

We see the signs of anticipatory grief – the inability to know or control an outcome – in this COVID World.

Where do we take it all?

Enter Jehovah Shammah. Look at God saying His name . . . I AM There.

Jehovah, derived from the Hebrew root, "to be, become." This name tells us He is totally self-existent – always has been, is, and always will be.

Also known as Yahweh – I AM.

Shammah – in Hebrew – is simply the word for "there."

Jehovah Shammah – I AM There.

See the beauty right now wherever it is you may find yourself . . . He is there.

You are NOT alone, unseen, unheard, abandoned, unknown.

Want to know how the faith giants, like Daniel, win the thing? Not only do they KNOW this with their "knower", they BELIEVE this with their "believer"!

Watch this. In a foreign land, as a young teen taken away from his family, being groomed by a foreign king for cultural greatness, mandated to forsake the customs and habits of his own culture and religion . . . Daniel KNOWS Jehovah Shammah.

The consistency of the habits Daniel had formed, provided the gateway into the presence of Jehovah Shammah Himself. Take a look at Daniel 6:10 NLT.

"But when Daniel learned that the law had been signed, he went home and knelt down *as usual* (emphasis mine) in his upstairs room, with its windows open toward Jerusalem. He prayed three times a day, *just as he had always done* (emphasis mine), giving thanks to his God."

After the King signs the edict that allows only for worship of himself, Daniel does what he did everyday – sets off to sit in the presence of Jehovah Shammah. See Daniel KNEW Jehovah Shammah would be there. Daniel KNEW because three times a day, for as long as Daniel could remember, Jehovah Shammah had been there. No edict could deter Daniel.

At a time when Daniel had every right to feel alone, unseen, unheard, abandoned, unknown, swallowed up in all the grief of his circumstances in a foreign land . . . Daniel didn't.

See, that consistent habit of meeting with Jehovah Shammah thrice daily, and carrying out Jehovah Shammah's mandates throughout the rest of the day is what prepared Daniel for the Lions' Den.

So today, Beloved, as you walk out all the uncertainty of these days, I am praying for you and for the habits of consistency you are forming. The times you are setting apart to strengthen your "KNOW" of Jehovah Shammah and to cement your "BELIEVING" that He is who He says is.

So when the grief is overwhelming and the earth shakes . . . you KNOW . . . I AM There is dwelling within you. You actually BELIEVE that His presence makes all the difference in your life.

Are you ready to lock arms with Him and win the day? If not, pray these prayers over yourself until you are.

Prayers of Affirmation

Jehovah Shammah, Today I choose You. Today I will direct all my attention and affection to You, for better is one day in Your courts than thousands elsewhere. Thank you, Lord, for making it possible for me to come into Your presence.

Scripture Reference: Psalm 84:10

Jehovah Shammah, Today let my greatest hunger and thirst be for Your Righteousness. In that quest I know I will be filled.
Scripture Reference: Matthew 5:6

Jehovah Shammah, Today I seek Your presence. For in that space You have made known to me the path of life. There is fullness of joy, and at Your right hand are treasures forever more.
Scripture Reference: Psalm 16:11

Come Up Higher Questions

1) Based on Hebrews 10:35–39, Where have I cast away my confidence in Your name here, Lord?

2) Where am I specifically drawing back in my knowledge of this name, Lord, purposefully not looking at things I need to see? Open my eyes to any blind spots I have to You regarding this name. Confess what He shows you.

3) Where specifically am I in need of endurance regarding this name, Lord?

4) What lies have I been believing about You pertaining to this name, Lord?
   What lies have I been believing about myself pertaining to this name, Lord?
   Confess those lies by writing them down in the journal pages and offer them back to Him.

5) Ask Him what truths He would like to replace those lies with regarding this name. Write those down in the journal pages that follow.

Today's Scripture Reference

"Therefore, do not throw away Your confidence, which has a great reward. For you have need of endurance, so that when you have done the will of God, you may receive what was promised. For yet in a very little while, He who is coming will come, and will not delay. But my righteous one shall live by faith; and if he shrinks back, my soul has no pleasure in him. But we are not of those who shrink back to destruction, but of those who have faith to the preserving of the soul." —Hebrews 10:35–39 NASB

Draw What's on Your Heart

Day Two

Your Invitation Awaits

Do you remember the excitement of getting ready for a party? Especially if you're the guest of honor . . . delightful.

How about receiving a college acceptance, a team draft, receiving an amazing job offer?

So many ways our earthly economy says, "Come on in . . . move up . . . it's time to promote and celebrate you."

An invitation to become a better version of yourself. To move up, be recognized and compensated for your hard work and efforts. That's good, right?

What about a crippling accident, a gut-wrenching, debilitating divorce, breast cancer, the loss of a business, loss of a spouse, abduction of a child, familial addiction, mental illness, death of a child . . .

God's invitations can look somehow grimly different at the outset . . . akin to a cruel joke perhaps.

Enter Jehovah Shammah. The Lord is There.

See here's the rub. In His economy, in the darkest of nights, Jehovah Shammah wants us to know one thing. One thing. He is there.

You are not alone for a nano-second. Not abandoned, not rejected. Not hung out to dry by some wicked higher being who causes these things to happen. NO!

What Jehovah Shammah wants you to know is that even though we live in a fallen world, it can never fall any further than He allows. And in the falling, Jehovah Shammah invites us in to experience MORE OF Himself. That MORE OF is ALWAYS GREATER THAN whatever the "invitation" is presenting.

In the darkest nights of the soul, Jehovah Shammah wants us to know that those are His specialty. The place where Jehovah Shammah thrives in the triumphant turnaround!

Jehovah Shammah promises us that He will give "beauty for ashes", a "joyous blessing instead of mourning" (Isaiah 61:3). He will "restore the years the locust have eaten" (Joel 2:25).

See the invitations in His economy far surpass the invitations of ours . . . if we can see past the initial horror of the thing. Jehovah Shammah's invitations invite us to become who He designed us to be . . . to fulfill the purposes He has created for us to fulfill . . . if we lean in for the learning.

I've lived enough of my own and seen the truth of it in the stories that come to me daily to know one thing. We can find Jehovah Shammah in the middle of the mess.

Jehovah Shammah is always there. Waiting with arms open wide to do the amazingly intricate work of putting us back together . . . His way.

So today, Beloved, it's my prayer for you that you would know Him in the middle of your darkest messes. That you would accept His invitation to come in and come higher in your relationship with Him.

See that's the thing . . . those messes . . . they're stepping stones for Jehovah Shammah. He is always far above them working all things together for good for you because you love Him and are called according to His purposes just as Paul told the Roman believers.

The question is, "Will you accept the invitation?" Beloved, my prayer is you will. Are you ready? If not, pray these prayers over yourself until you are.

Prayers of Affirmation

Jehovah Shammah, Today I choose You. I accept Your invitation to draw close to You. Your promises are my armor and protection. I am covered with Your feathers, and have found my refuge under Your wings.
Scripture Reference: Psalm 91:4

Jehovah Shammah, You are here. I am not alone. Today, I receive Your beauty for my ashes. I receive a joyous blessing instead of mourning. Today I rise up above what I can see to receive the promises of Your Word. Your Word is truth.
Scripture Reference: Isaiah 61:3

Jehovah Shammah, Thank you for the promises of Your Word. They are true. Today I stand on them. I thank you that You are working all things together for my good because I love You, and I am called according to Your purposes.

Scripture Reference: Romans 8:28

Come Up Higher Questions

1) Lord, would You give me an opportunity to apply the knowledge of this name in my life today?

2) Lord, can You show me what You see in my applying this name today?

3) Lord, can You show me the treasure that You have placed in this person / situation in which I will be applying this name today?

4) What lies have I believed here that I need to break agreement with today in regard to this name / person / situation?

5) What truths do I need to replace those lies with?

Today's Scripture Reference

"But prove yourselves doers of the word, and not merely hearers who delude themselves. For if anyone is a hearer of the word and not a doer, he is like a man who looks at his natural face in a mirror; for once he has looked at himself and gone away, he has immediately forgotten what kind of person he was. But one who looks intently at the perfect law, and law of liberty, and abides by it, not having become a forgetful hearer but an effectual doer, this man will be blessed in what he does."

—James 1:22–25 NASB

Jehovah Shammah

Your Invitation Awaits

Draw What's on Your Heart

Day Three

Gifting the Giver

WHAT GIFT DOES ONE GIVE to the Ultimate Giver? What creation can I construct for the Creator Himself? How do I bless My Beloved?

Have you ever wondered?

Perhaps we can glean a thing or two from the much-speculated, unnamed woman in Luke 7 (go check her story out there).

Let's start here at what she offers Him . . .

At great expense to herself to even show up to the party, she risked (and received) scorn, indignation, shame, condemnation, judgment from those in attendance. It was worth the risk to her.

Why, you may ask? Because Jehovah Shammah. Where He was, she knew she needed to be.

First Gift . . . She stood confidently against her accusers, as she sat at Jesus' feet and offered Him her presence, at great cost to herself.

Second Gift . . . Her alabaster jar of anointing oil that she used on Jesus was worth a year's wages . . . a YEAR'S wages! To say, in that patriarchal economy, that she gave sacrificially, would be an understatement. And still she was chastised by the educated, men of stature in her presence.

Third Gift . . . amidst the discussion of her own worthiness and that of her gift, Jehovah Shammah speaks, coming to her defense. No wonder she wanted to be where He was. She offers Jehovah Shammah her worship. Each action of hers on behalf of Jehovah Shammah – her breaking open and pouring out her most valuable possession on Jesus' feet, her tears, her wiping Jesus' feet with her hair, her posture at Jesus' feet. These things all say . . . You are here. You are worthy. I am willing.

So today, let's do the John 6:29 work of believing that Jehovah Shammah is who He says He is, no matter the opposition or cost.

So today, Beloved, it is my prayer for you that you open the costly alabaster jar of Jehovah Shammah's word and pour out these truths as you anoint yourself with what Jehovah Shammah has to say to and about you. This is the truth. Repeat it till you believe it. While you're at it, here's a thing to think through . . .

It is discussed that this brave soul was one accustomed to sitting at Jesus' feet. That we may have seen her before occupying that same space in Luke 10 . . . with her sister, Martha. I'll let you go study that out.

Are you ready? If not, pray these prayers over yourself until you are.

Prayers of Affirmation

Jehovah Shammah, Today I receive and stand firmly planted in Your eternal presence through the gift of the Holy Spirit. Thank you that through the gift of the Holy Spirit I am assured that I will never be alone.
Scripture Reference: Deuteronomy 31:6

Jehovah Shammah, Thank you that because You are here I know that I need not fear. You are orchestrating my way out safely. In the meantime, You help me to stand firm against my fiercest enemies.
Scripture Reference: Isaiah 40:3–5

Jehovah Shammah, I receive the comfort of Your presence that extends even into the darkest valleys of my life. Even in those places I know that I am not alone, You are with me. Your rod and Your staff are there for my protection.
Scripture Reference: Psalm 23:4

Come Up Higher Questions

1) How do I love You in truth today, Lord, in regard to this name?

2) Ask God if He can show you how to love yourself the way He loves you specifically in regard to this name.

3) In what tangible ways can I partner with this name of God to manifest Your presence more clearly in my daily life today, Lord?

4) What gift or talent (equipment or fruit of the Spirit) do I need to manifest this name of Yours on earth today, Lord?

5) Lord, is there anything more You would like to reveal to me about this name?

Today's Scripture Reference

"For the testimony of Jesus is the spirit of prophecy."
—Revelation 19:10b NASB

"But the fruit of the Spirit is love, joy, peace, patience, kindness, goodness, faithfulness, gentleness, self-control; against such things there is no law."
—Galatians 5:22-23 NASB

> "... Jehovah Shammah. Where He was,
> she knew she needed to be."
> —Dawn E. Stephenson, *Who Do You Say I Am?*

Jehovah Shammah

Gifting the Giver

Draw What's on Your Heart

Day Four

A Series of Unfortunate Events

I picked up the phone and heard, "This is the Office of the President at (insert big office supply company name) My name is ———." Seems I had been heard. I had been walking through a "textbook customer service" issue with a missing, delayed, mishandled order over the past week with this company . . . spoken to many levels of management and even their training team! Each encounter consumed approximately, on average, an hour. Be careful if you ever pray for patience.

Each step of the way, lots of promises, but ultimately, in a "series of unfortunate events" (as I termed this experience), the order missed two promised delivery dates, including one delivery to a wrong address 1,000 miles away. All that to say, the things I was counting on, and in need of . . . not there. I kept waiting . . . to no avail. Until finally today when the doorbell rang. There it was.

Unlike Jehovah Shammah. He's simply always there.

I don't have to hunt Jehovah Shammah down, I don't have to work hard with no return, I don't have to wonder if He'll ever get here . . .

His name is His nature. Jehovah Shammah is here.

The consummate gentleman, Jehovah Shammah simply is waiting for us to extend the invitation to let Him in. To let Jehovah Shammah deliver His promises to us. Jehovah Shammah died for the privilege to do so.

What if my package was like that? What if, on the first call, while I was still talking to the Customer Service Rep, I opened the door and there was the delivery. That's Jehovah Shammah. "The eyes of the Lord search the whole earth in order to strengthen those whose hearts are fully committed to Him." II Chronicles 16:9 NLT.

Jehovah Shammah stands waiting to bring heaven to earth for us. To partner with us in healing, in redemption, in restoration, in reconciliation. We call and show up in obedience, and Jehovah Shammah begins immediate delivery on the process of creating our "abundant life" He died for us to have HERE on earth. That's not a promise reserved just for heaven. Jehovah Shammah brings that part of heaven here for us to enjoy as we walk with Him daily.

While I am truly grateful for the call from the president of the company, the free order, and the free coupons that will last a year . . . that all pales in comparison to Jehovah Shammah.

That's my prayer for you today, Beloved, that you avail yourselves of the riches and abundance, wholeness and healing of Jehovah Shammah. That you don't, for a second, walk this journey alone. Jehovah Shammah died so you don't have to. Can you trust Jehovah Shammah sight unseen, heart fully committed? He is there.

Are you ready? Speak these prayers over yourself until you can.

Prayers of Affirmation

Jehovah Shammah, You are here. I am not alone. You are a wall of fire around me and the Spirit within me. I welcome You in to walk with me and bring me into the fullness of who You created me to be.
Scripture Reference: Zechariah 2:5

Jehovah Shammah, You have said You are with us always, even until the end of the age. Thank you that I will never walk alone.
Scripture Reference: Matthew 28:20

Jehovah Shammah, You have promised healing and abundant life. I stand ready to walk that out with You, hand in hand. Today I thank you that I am NEVER alone . . . not for one nano-second.
Scripture Reference: John 10:10

Come Up Higher Questions

1) How can I use this name of God to bring the kingdom of heaven to earth today, Lord?

2) How does this name of God contribute to the flourishing of my neighbors and city, Lord?

3) Lord, can You give me an encouraging word for another regarding this particular name through picture, scripture, song, or word?

4) Ask Him for any further clarification on the above word that He would like to share with you. Write it down. Share these words with that person.

5) Lord, what would You like to say to me today regarding this name that might encourage my own heart? Write it down.

Today's Scripture Reference

"Your kingdom come, Your will be done on earth as it is in heaven."
—Matthew 6:10 NASB

"Behold, I will do something new, now it will spring forth; will you not be aware of it? I will even make a roadway in the wilderness, rivers in the desert."
—Isaiah 43:19 NASB

Jehovah Shammah

A Series of Unfortunate Events

Draw What's on Your Heart

Day Five

The Victory Lap

I don't know if sitting in a hospital parking lot, up on the observation deck, in the dark at 5:15 a.m., taking makeshift communion of Gatorade and Ritz crackers to fuel the seven lap (9,000 plus step) hospital campus prayer walk you were about to embark on, is your idea of fun; but if it is, thank Jehovah Shammah!

Here's the thing. When we let love lead, it takes us to some crazy places to execute some really far out ideas . . . those directly from the mind of Jehovah Shammah Himself. Believe me when I tell you, when you get that "marching order" you don't want to be anywhere else, because well . . . Jehovah Shammah – The Lord (Himself) is There!

Such was the morning when my warrior Christ Sister and her dear friend were led to that spot to begin the Joshua 6 Victory March around the hospital campus. Six times around to cover the surgery that was about to happen on one of her church leaders. Then the seventh lap was the "Victory Lap"! March they did! Got to see and shout to their friend from the parking deck as her car arrived at the hospital, got to minister to a gal who was waiting at a bus station having recently been discharged, all while walking and praying. All covered by Jehovah Shammah. Glorious.

"NO CANCER!" was the purpose of this march and victory cry on the seventh lap around.

With that they set off for a well-earned hearty breakfast.

Fast forward ten days, when the lab reports came back with not a cell of cancer in the removal sight or any one of the twenty-five surrounding lymph nodes . . . much to the surprise of the doctors and surgeons. So much so, they questioned doing the surgery.

But not to my friend and her prayer partner. There was no surprise there! Just a confirmation of what happens when we go where He calls us, Jehovah Shammah. Even if it is to a hospital parking deck at 5 a.m.

Because it is in that space we will get to have the privilege of partnering with Jehovah Shammah. Because The Lord is There, and He's inviting you along on the adventure!

That's my prayer for you today, Beloved. That you would take the risk when He plants the crazy idea . . . whatever it is, wherever it takes you. Because that is where you will certainly find Jehovah Shammah waiting for you. Are you ready? If not, speak these prayers over yourself until you are.

Prayers of Affirmation

Jehovah Shammah, I want to be where You are doing what You have planned for me to do. Lord, give me the desire and will of Joshua who would not leave the tent of meeting because his desire for You made the world around him fade away.
Scripture Reference: Exodus 33:11

Jehovah Shammah, Today I receive the invitation to be where You are, because it is in that space that I find my rest in You.
Scripture Reference: Mark 6:31

Jehovah Shammah, Speak, Your servant hears. I will follow You all the days of my life led by Your goodness and mercy until I dwell in Your house forever.
Scripture Reference: I Samuel 3:10, Psalm 23:6

Come Up Higher Questions

1) Lord, what is the heart of this name of God towards me today?

2) Lord, is there anything else about the heart of this name of God towards me that I need to know or do today?

3) Lord, is there any area in my life in regard to this name in which I am out of obedience or susceptible to sin? Confess that area in the journal space provided.

4) Lord, what is the gift that You desire to give me in place of that area of weakness or disobedience that I can use to build Your kingdom?

5) Lord, what aspect of Your character or nature would You like to show me, in regard to this name, that I have not seen before?

Today's Scripture Reference

"Therefore there is now no condemnation for those who are in Christ Jesus."
—Romans 8:1 NASB

"What then shall we say to these things? If God is for us, who is against us? He who did not spare His own Son, but delivered Him over for us all, how will He not also with Him freely give us all things?"
—Romans 8:31–32 NASB

"If we confess our sins, He is faithful and righteous to forgive us our sins and to cleanse us from all unrighteousness."
—I John 1:9 NASB

Jehovah Shammah

The Victory Lap

Draw What's on Your Heart

Triumphing Through Trauma

Introduction to Exercises

THE ABILITY TO TRIUMPH THROUGH TRAUMA takes much courage, and it always lies far on the other side of our comfort zones. To come into a healthy reality is a painstaking journey and entails much maintenance amongst the right others to maintain the course. It is often gritty and messy to dig into the pain of the past. Yet, despite all of that, I cannot think of a thing that brings more glory and honor to every name of God than doing just that.

As Hebrews 5:14 NIV so brilliantly points out, "But solid food is for the mature, *who by constant use have trained themselves* to distinguish good from evil." (emphasis mine)

The spiritually mature are those who "constantly train themselves to distinguish good from evil."

God will be tender and gracious as you press in for healing. His voice is always encouraging as He gently leads us out of our dysfunction into our healing.

As Romans 2:4 NLT tells us, "Can't you see that His kindness is meant to lead you to repentance?"

I have included several exercises that God spoke into my own heart as He did the glorious, transformational healing work in it.

It is my hope that you might find them equally as helpful.

Never Alone & Confessional

> "In failing to confess, Lord, I would only hide
> You from myself, not myself from You."
> —Saint Augustine

It is important to know in our "knower", and more importantly to believe in our "believer" that we are never alone. Our God sees. God is interested, God is invested, God has His Son's skin, yes, even life, in the game of your life.

Not only are we seen, we are known, loved, cherished by Him. In a way that should leave us in awe. In that arena, it would be in our best interest to keep our accounts short with God – to let Him gently and lovingly correct us and bring us back to Himself when we have gone astray.

Here is an exercise that acknowledges God's omnipresence but also His very present presence in my life, while at the same time inviting God into the very sacred space of confession. Take some time to draw away with the Lord to that space by repeating this beautiful psalm, Psalm 139, of David.

Psalm 139
For the choir director: A Psalm of David (NLT)

V.1 O Lord (YHWH), You have examined my heart and know everything about me.

V.2 You know when I sit down or stand up. You know my thoughts even when I'm far away.

V.3 You see me when I travel and when I rest at home. You know everything I do.

V.4 You know what I am going to say even before I say it, Lord.

V. 5 You go before me and follow me. You place your hand of blessing on my head.

V. 6 Such knowledge is too wonderful for me, too great for me to understand!

V. 7 I can never escape from your Spirit! I can never get away from your presence!

V. 8 If I go up to heaven, you are there; if I go down to the grave, you are there.

V. 9 If I ride the wings of the morning, if I dwell by the farthest oceans,

V. 10 even there your hand will guide me, and your strength will support me.

V. 11 I could ask the darkness to hide me and the light around me to become night –

V. 12 but even in darkness I cannot hide from you. To you the night shines as bright as day. Darkness and light are the same to you.

V. 13 You made all the delicate, inner parts of my body and knit me together in my mother's womb.

V. 14 Thank you for making me so wonderfully complex! Your workmanship is marvelous – how well I know it.

V. 15 You watched me as I was being formed in utter seclusion, as I was woven together in the dark of the womb.

V. 16 You saw me before I was born. Every day of my life was recorded in Your book. Every moment was laid out before a single day had passed.

V. 17 How precious are your thoughts about me, O God. They cannot be numbered!

V. 18 I can't even count them; they outnumber the grains of sand!
And when I wake up, You are still with me!

V. 19 O God, if only You would destroy the wicked! Get out of my life, you murderers!

V. 20 They blaspheme You; Your enemies misuse Your name.
V. 21 O Lord, shouldn't I hate those who hate You? Shouldn't I despise those who oppose you?

V. 22 Yes, I hate them with total hatred, for Your enemies are my enemies.

Psalm 139:23-24
The Confessional

V. 23 Search me, O God, and know my heart; test me and know my anxious thoughts.

V. 24 Point out anything in me that offends You, and lead me along the path of everlasting life.

Overcoming with the Names of God

A key to overcoming is time in the presence of God Himself. It cannot be shortcut, nor is there a hack on overcoming or getting to spiritual maturity.

Jesus said it best this way: "Come away with Me to a secret place and rest awhile." Mark 6:31

It is in that space that we can offer Him our full affection and our full attention. We can form a strategic partnership that allows an uninterrupted flow of communication. There is a dialogue. He welcomes our questions.

It is in this space that He can lead us to healing:

1) Declare to Holy Spirit that you would like to partner with Him in the area in which you are seeking healing
2) Ask Him to reveal any unhealthy partnerships or alliances that you have formed with the enemy either by choice or through generational sin
3) Topically research the subject biblically looking for cause and effect, threads, and ways that the biblical character overcame

4) Set your flesh, soul, spirit in firm resolution of obedience to walk out this new Godly partnership
5) Take ownership of any thoughts that are contrary to biblical truth and renounce them to God as lies
6) Take authority over your flesh by declaring, "I command you to come into alignment and agreement with the Word of God and His authority in my life. Flesh align through the authority Christ died for me to have over sin."

Action Points

Pray
Make scriptural declarations of truth
Set boundaries
Be honest with God
Take up the weapon of obedience

Laying a Firm Foundation

Oftentimes overcoming leads us to have to start over in many arenas. From the littlest to the largest areas of life, sometimes these processes can cause us to feel like we are navigating unfamiliar, uncharted territory. They can be confusing and perhaps become daunting and overwhelming.

It was during one of those reorganization periods that the Lord lovingly stepped in and gave me a rubric called Laying a Firm Foundation.

In typical ABBA fashion, He also gave me a scripture that I find myself gravitating to during uncertain times. Hopefully, it will provide you with the same comfort I found.

I Am With You
Adapted from Isaiah 42 (MSG)

"Don't worry (insert your name), I'll take your hand because you don't know the way.
You can't see where you are going.
I will be your personal guide directing you through unknown country.
I'll be right there to show you what roads to take and make sure that you don't fall into a ditch.
These are the things I'll be doing for you.
I'll be sticking with you, not leaving you for a minute."
Love You,
ABBA

Laying A Firm Foundation

S.A.M.E.
S: Simplify every area of life
A: Annihilate loose ends
M: Make the most of what you have
E: Work with excellence

Simplify Every Area of Life – It is easiest when we can take control of chaos by removing the extraneous clutter from our lives and minds. To live minimally allows our minds to focus on what is important and heal from trauma.

Downsizing, streamlining systems, decluttering, surrounding ourselves with only things that matter, and living below our means allows us to recoup and regroup into healthier places much quicker.

Annihilate Loose Ends – Part of taking control of chaos often involves having to rebuild in many areas of life. This often takes many years. Start with the most important areas first as you can handle them. Small tasks that you can finish build confidence. Give yourself many kudos each time something is accomplished.

Make the Most of What You Have – While easily overlooked this is an important step. In conjunction with simplifying life, decluttering, and making space, this step has helped me to become much more aware of life in terms of budgeting, and taking inventory of material things in general. It helps to find multiple use items in order to facilitate the goal of keeping things simple. The old saying from WWII has proven useful here: "Use it up, wear it out, make it do, or do without!"

Work with Excellence – To finalize the above, the concept of excellence has moved to the forefront. Once in healthier spaces, there is no longer a need to accept every invitation, jump into every service position, or volunteer at every event. It is beautiful to be able to stop running and enjoy the healthy simplicity of a newly created life with margin. The ability to focus on excellence as a core life value then allows us to work from a position of intentional excellence with purpose on the things that are of extreme value to us. These are things chosen that will support our purpose, ministry, and calling. All done with the excellent caliber of which they are worthy. Simply said it's the old adage of "quality versus quantity."

A New Name

In ancient Hebrew culture your name had very strong connotations that were attached to you directly. They took the whole naming process very seriously. The actual Hebrew word for name in Genesis 2:7 means "breath." In essence, a "name" is a person's "breath", their character.

So we see in biblical times, when God desired to do a mighty work in someone, He would also change their name to match the "new" person and mission He was creating in them and for them to fulfill.

Take, for example, Abram. God changed his name to Abraham. He went from "exalted father" to "father of a multitude." His name now reflected God's purpose for his life. How about Sarai (quarrelsome)? She went to Sarah (My Princess, noblewoman). How much more accurately did her new name match God's vision for her life?

After looking at all of God's names, God had me look at my own. Now, I had always had a severe disdain for my name for all the pain and brokenness that was attached to it from childhood. That was until God showed me a new way to look at it. I would encourage you to look at your name as well . . . since we are on the subject!

My first name, Dawn, means "from the breaking of the day, the one who breaks through darkness."

My middle name, Elizabeth, means "consecrated one, or consecrated to."

Then one day the Lord showed me that He is victorious . . . always. That God has given to us all that belongs to His Son including His victorious nature (Philippians 4:13). Through Christ, we can consistently walk in His victorious nature! How exciting!! So I took a look at it and put it all together. That was the day I went from disdaining my name to loving it. My name was now my nature. Take a look!

Dawn – From the breaking of the day.
One who breaks through darkness.

Elizabeth – Consecrated to Victory / to be Victorious –
One who is characterized by victory

Do you see it, Beloved?

From the breaking of the day, I am the one who (in His power and authority) breaks through darkness to be victorious (meaning to be characterized by victory)!

What a glorious transformation.

Isn't Holy Spirit fun? I'll take that and walk in it!

I would encourage you to spend some time in God's presence asking Him about your name. I would encourage you to ask God how He sees you. What God's plans are for you. Look at what your given names mean. Ask God how they fit into His plans for you for the future. The ones God tells us He has for us, to give us a future and a hope (Jeremiah 29:11). Wait to see what God shows you what He's thinking!

Crisis Resources

The following is a list of resources that I have either used personally or know of through my own research in healing with crises and trauma in my own life. They are typically classified under an evangelical, biblical worldview. Please either use them yourself, if you find yourself in that place, or know someone who is.

Leslie Vernick, *The Emotionally Destructive Marriage*, *The Emotionally Destructive Relationship*, CONQUER Group www.leslievernick.com

Dr. Henry Cloud, *Boundaries, Boundaries in Marriage, Changes that Heal, Necessary Endings*, Churches that Heal Program www.drcloud.com

Shannon Thomas, *Healing from Hidden Abuse, Exposing Financial Abuse* www.shannonthomas.com

Give Her Wings – A non-profit (501c3) organization that helps and serves single mothers who have left abusive relationships and have little to no recourse. Bringing help, hope, and healing to these amazing moms. www.giveherwings.com

Consumer Credit Counseling Services (CCCS) – a 45-year old non-profit credit counseling service agency under the NFCC. They are an Internal Revenue Services (IRS) 501(c)(3) non-profit organization that will help you find a workable solution to financial problems including financial education, budgeting assistance, and debt management plans. www.credit.org

Bethel Church Sozo Ministry – Sozo is a healing and deliverance ministry that was founded and run by Dawna De Silva and Teresa Liebscher out of

Bethel Church in Redding, CA. Sozo (Greek) for saved, healed, delivered, is a unique inner healing and deliverance ministry aimed to get to the root of things hindering your personal connection with Father God, Son, and Holy Spirit. This powerfully anointed healing group offers sessions and additionally has trained teams globally in this ministry. Search their website for further information. www.bethelsozo.com

NOTE: This list of resources/recommendations is not intended to be used as professional advice nor as an endorsement/guarantee of services offered by listed resources. They are offered as a starting point for your own research. In the course of my own personal journey, these exercises/resources were helpful so I am sharing them with you.

Acknowledgements

Every book we hold in our hands bears testimony of one's tribe at work. This is no exception, and I am eternally grateful for mine.

To be a part of the body of Christ functioning as intended truly lifts a soul into the presence of God Himself. It serves to remind us that heaven is truly going to be beyond our grasp. In the meanwhile, a huge thank you to the following people for bringing a slice of it down to earth as we labored together to bring this project to fruition.

First and foremost, if there were a trillion names for God, I will never tire of sitting in His presence. Thank you, Lord, for all the rescuing, restoring, and redeeming You've done in my life. You make the most excellent of Husbands. I am My Beloved's, and My Beloved is mine. More than anything, thank you for lavishing me with the gift of my belovedness. I treasure it as dearly as life itself.

To the Prayer Warriors that covered this project. Thank you for being my Aaronnesses and Hurs, for lifting my arms when the battles raged. In the midst of a snowstorm, a tropical storm, COVID-19, an election, many other battles too lengthy to mention . . . it is each of you who ensured the victory in the form of the book that you hold in your hands. It is a privilege to call you not only Frontline Warriors, but treasured friends. I will forever be grateful to walk the front lines with Barb Hollace, Kathleen Hoffman and Lorrie Roe.

To my NCC Upper Zoom Family, thank you for restoring my faith in the body of Christ. What a gift you are! You effuse love, stand for justice, build bridges over divides, think with the minds of solutionaries, and challenge us to move far outside of our comfort zones. Throughout 2020, you have been a constant reminder that we can face big problems with bold faith. My anchor holds because of this group!

Lastly, to my children and their families: Anthony, Elizabeth, Elijah, Ezekiel, Glenn Jr., Melissa, Daniel, and Olivia. It is you all who have kept me centered in the darkest of days. Thank you for serving, always, as a reminder that no matter what . . . LOVE WINS! I love you all to the moon and back . . . and then some!

About the Author

AFTER THIRTY YEARS IN RECOVERY and triumphing over 90 percent of the Top Life Stressor List in the past ten years, Dawn Stephenson has chosen to use these experiences as the training ground for the next generation of spiritual Frontline Warriors.

Dawn is an entrepreneur and published author who loves to write, mentor, coach, teach, and speak all things Jesus. Her passion for philanthropy and development has found her sitting on boards, both locally and nationally.

On the daily, Dawn is the CEO and Founder of Platinum Travel Insiders, her boutique, luxury management travel firm located in the New York / New Jersey Metropolitan area and Turks & Caicos.

Additionally, Dawn is the Founder of Kairos Coaching and Consulting, where she gets to execute her passion of speaking life and healing into the Bride of Christ through speaking, consulting, educating lay leaders on liberating the evangelically oppressed.

Dawn is the mom to her tribe of four (two married) and Queenie to two grand princes. When she is not battling on the frontlines, you can find Dawn decompressing with marine life under a turquoise sea, working on her Belonger Status in Turks & Caicos, or home in the Southeast with her kitty, Mia.

Author's Note

I HAVE LEARNED IN THE SACRED SPACE of the past five years that God is too kind to waste any of our pain and suffering. The book you hold in your hands is proof of that very thing.

Pressing into Him, holding on like Joshua in Exodus 17:8–16, refusing to leave my chair, aka my own Tent of Meeting. The pain too great, the presence of God Himself too powerful. God was teaching me a new way through. I needed to learn God at an entirely different level to battle in the spaces to which He was calling me. This was front-line warfare. I was to become a Frontline Warrior. I relied heavily on His promise that I rewrote from Isaiah 42:16 MSG. Personalized, it reads like this:

"But I'll take your hand, Dawn, because you don't know the way. You can't see where you're going. I'll be a personal guide to you, directing you through unknown country. I'll be right there to show you what roads to take, to make sure you don't fall into the ditch. These are the things I'll do for you – sticking with you, not leaving you for a minute."

I can't tell you how valuable those words became to me. So I share them with you wherever you find yourself on your journey to wholeness. Because to rise victoriously into our calling ensures that we will battle on the front lines.

Pastor Mark Batterson of National Community Church in Washington, DC, calls this "flipping the blessing" . . . or the Double Blessing. We are blessed to bless others. It's leveraging the blessing.

So today, Beloved, that is my gift to you – this book, this promise . . . the leveraged blessing that brought me to my belovedness and taught me how to walk there. May it do the same for you.

"'But what about you?' He (Jesus) asked. 'Who do you say I am?'"
—Mark 8:29

Made in the USA
Middletown, DE
11 April 2025